DISUSED STA
Closed Railway Stations In the UK

Lost Stations of North West England

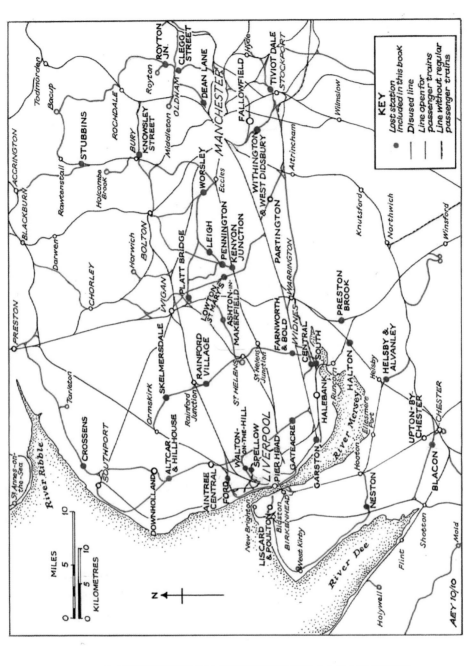

KEY

● Lost station included in this book
— Disused line
— Line open for passenger trains
-- Line without regular passenger trains

MILES
5 10

KILOMETRES
5 10

N ←

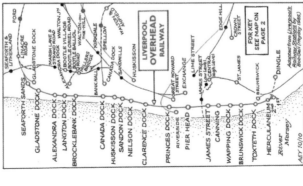

LIVERPOOL OVERHEAD RAILWAY

FOR KEY SEE MAP ON PAGE 2

SEAFORTH SANDS
GLADSTONE DOCK
ALEXANDRA DOCK
LANGTON DOCK
BROCKLEBANK DOCK
CANADA DOCK
HUSKISSON DOCK
SANDON DOCK
NELSON DOCK
CLARENCE DOCK
PRINCES DOCK
RIVERSIDE
PIER HEAD
JAMES STREET
CANNING
WAPPING DOCK
BRUNSWICK DOCK
TOXTETH DOCK
HERCULANEUM
River Mersey

Adapted from *Liverpool Railway Stations* by Bob Gent (Mighty Ride)

AEY 10/10

Lost Stations of
North West England

Paul Wright

Silver Link Publishing Ltd

First published in 2011

British Library Cataloguing in Publication Data

A catalogue record for this book is available from the
British Library.

ISBN 978 1 85794 371 9

Silver Link Publishing Ltd
The Trundle
Ringstead Road
Great Addington
Kettering
Northants NN14 4BW

Tel/Fax: 01536 330588
email: sales@nostalgiacollection.com
Website: www.nostalgiacollection.com

Printed and bound in the Czech Republic

Please note:
Silver Link Publishing Ltd (Silver Link) is not responsible for the content of external websites. The reasons for this are as follows:

> Silver Link does not produce them or maintain/update them
> and cannot change them.
> Such sites can be changed without Silver Link's knowledge or
> agreement.

Where external links are given they may be to websites which also offer commercial services, such as online purchasing. The inclusion of
a link or links to a website(s) in our books should not be taken or understood to be an endorsement of any kind of that website(s) or the
site's owners, their products or services.

The Author - Paul Wright

Paul Wright was born in Wallasey in 1964 into
a Liverpool family. His childhood coincided
with a sharp decline in the fortunes of Britain's
railways. In 1965 he moved to Widnes, a
small industrial town that could once boast
eight active passenger stations, two of which
were within a short walk of the author's
home. With regular Saturday and school
holiday visits to Grandparents in the Walton
area of Liverpool there were plenty of railway
locations where the author could play and
explore during the 1970s and this awakened a
fascination in the subject.

Since 1986 Paul has enjoyed a career in Local
Government working within Public Parks,
currently being employed by Halton Borough
Council as the head of their Open Space
Services. Interestingly he now has responsibility
for many of the former railway sites on which
he used to play as they have over the years
been developed as public open spaces.

In 1989 Paul moved back to Wallasey and since
1991 he has been a serving Crew Member with
the RNLI's New Brighton Station and currently
holds the rank of Hovercraft Commander.

In 2005 Paul discovered Nick Catford's Closed
Stations Website and sent in some of his
material for inclusion. The result was that he
became a contributor to the site concentrating
on the North West and North Wales area.
Since 2005 he has contributed material for
hundreds of stations that are now on the
website.

Paul is also a keen motorcyclist, enjoys music,
cinema, running and the study of his family
history.

Contents

Acknowledgements

I would like to thank Nick Catford for starting the Disused Stations website, which has become such a popular railway history site and has led to the publication of this book. Thanks also to Nick for his assistance with the preparation of maps and pictures. Thanks to Alan Young for drawing the overall map, and to Peter Townsend of Silver Link Publishing for encouraging the idea of a companion book to the website.

Ordnance Survey deserves a special mention, as without its fine products both past and present the survey work and presentation of closed station information, both on the website and in the book, would not have the clarity that it does.

I would also like to thank the following for their help with the research that went into preparing this book: Paul Bolger, Tony Graham, Richard Mercer, Bevan Price, and Phil Williams. Thanks also to all those photographers whose foresight and effort has enabled me to illustrate the 31 station sites so clearly.

Bibliography

Anderson, P. *An Illustrated History of Liverpool's Railways* (Irwell Press, 1996)

Awdry, C. *Encyclopaedia of British Railway Companies* (Patrick Stephens Ltd, 1990)

Bolger, P. *Merseyside & District Railway Stations* (The Bluecoat Press, 1994)
The Cheshire Lines Railway: An Illustrated History

Clinker, C. R. and Firth, J. M. *Clinker's Register of Closed Passenger Stations and Goods Depots in England, Scotland & Wales 1830-1970* (C. R. Clinker, 1971)

Fox, G. K. *Scenes from the Past 13A: Stockport Tiviot Dale – a Cheshire line remembered* (Foxline, 2008; first edition, 1991)

Gahan, J. W. *Seaport to Seaside* (Countryvise, 1985)
Seventeen Stations to Dingle (Countryvise, 1982)

Gell, R. *An Illustrated Survey of Railway Stations between Southport and Liverpool* (Heyday Publishing, 1986)

Johnson, E. M. *Scenes from the Past 16: The Midland Route from Manchester – Part One, Central to New Mills via Didsbury, Stockport & Marple* (Foxline)

Hall, S. *Rail Centres: Manchester* (Ian Allan, 1995)

LMS Summer Timetable, 18 July to 11 September 1932

Marshall, J. *The Lancashire & Yorkshire Railway* (Volume 1: David & Charles, 1969; Volume 2: David & Charles, 1970)

Maund, T. B. *Merseyrail Electrics: The Inside Story* (NBC Books, 2001)
The Wirral Railway and its Predecessors (Lightmoor Press, 2009)

Oppitz, L. *Lost Railways of Cheshire* (Countryside Books, 1997)

Tolston, J. M. *The St Helens Railway* (Oakwood Press, 1983)

Introduction

People have always had a fascination with disused railway lines and stations. Ever since the opening of the first railway lines in the 1820s, stations have been closing, many in the last century because they were resited to more suitable locations. This is particularly true in London, where many of the London termini were originally built some distance short of their present site.

In the early 20th century, stations and lines began to close with the introduction of new bus services, the increased popularity of the car and the improvements in roads. Other lines and stations never lived up to the expectations of their promoters.

Many rural stations were badly sited, well away from the towns and villages they were designed to serve, and this too led to a rapid decline in passenger numbers when more convenient forms of transport became available.

The steady trickle of railway closures increased in the 1950s, turning into a torrent in the 1960s with the rationalisation of our railway network under the infamous Dr Richard Beeching, Chairman of British Railways from 1961 to 1965.

In March 1963 his report *The Reshaping of British Railways* was published. The 'Beeching Axe', as it became known, proposed a massive closure programme. He recommended the closure of one-third of Britain's 18,000-mile railway network, mainly rural branches and cross-country lines, and 2,128 stations on lines that were to be kept open. The following year his second report, *The Development of the Major Railway Trunk Routes*, was even more scathing with a proposal that all lines should be closed apart from the major intercity routes and important profit-making commuter lines around the big cities, leaving Britain with little more than a skeleton railway system and large parts of the country entirely devoid of railways. The report was rejected by the Government and Dr Beeching resigned in 1965.

Although Beeching was gone, the closure programme that he started under the Conservatives in the early 1960s continued unabated under Labour until it was brought to a halt in the early 1970s, but by that time the damage had been done. In 1955 the British railway system consisted of 20,000 miles of track and 6,000 stations. By 1975 this had shrunk to 12,000 miles of track and 2,000 stations, roughly the same size it is today. Although there have been closures after 1975, they have tended to be balanced by reopenings.

Gradually the memory of these lost lines and stations began to fade as the urban sites were redeveloped, with only a road name to remind people of their former existence. Most of the rural sites were returned to nature and agriculture, although many of the stations still survive in some form or another, some transformed into attractive country dwellings while others linger on in the undergrowth, abandoned and forgotten.

In 2004 Nick Catford, a member of Subterranea Britannica,

Townley, C. H. A. and Peden, J. A. *Industrial Railways of St Helens, Widnes and Warrington*, Part 1 (Industrial Railway Society, 1999)

Pixton, B. *Widnes and St Helens Railways* (Chalford, 1996)

Quick, M. *Railway Passenger Stations in Great Britain* (RCHS, 2009)

Shannon, P. and Hillmer, J. *British Railways Past and Present No 3: The North West* (Silver Link Publishing, 1991)
British Railways Past and Present No 39: Liverpool and Wirral (Past & Present Publishing, 2002)
British Railways Past and Present No 40: Cheshire (Past & Present Publishing, 2003)
British Railways Past and Present No 41: Manchester and South Lancashire (Past & Present Publishing, 2003)

Suggitt, G. *Lost Railways of Merseyside and Greater Manchester* (Countryside Books, 2004)

Sweeney, D. J. *A Lancashire Triangle*, Part 2 (Triangle Publishing, 1997)

Wells, J. *Railways in and around Bury* (Booklaw/Railbus Publications, 2006)
Scenes from the Past 42: The Oldham Loop – Part 1, Manchester Victoria to Shaw and Crompton (Foxline, 2002)

Wells, J. and Bentley, E. *Scenes from the Past 33: East Lancashire Lines, Bury to Heywood and Rawtenstall* (Foxline, 2007)

Wright, P. *Disused Stations: Lost Stations of North West England* (Silver Link Publishing, 2010)
The Widnes to St Helens Railway in Halton 1833-1982 (Halton Borough Council, 2008)

Back issues of *Railway World* magazine

started the Disused Stations website with the aim of creating a definitive database of the UK's closed stations that would be available free to all. The work to complete the database is still ongoing and will take many years to complete. To date there are 1,510 stations on the site and it is visited by thousands of people every week.

This book is the second in a series that is intended to act as a companion to the Disused Stations website. It follows roughly the same format as the website but, as a book, it should appeal to those who want to have something tangible to put on their bookshelf, and it should also appeal to those who want to go out and visit the sites of the stations as it can be used as a guide book.

I have chosen a selection of stations from a variety of different lines, and they appear here in chronological order of opening. I felt that this would be a good way of showing how the network developed, expanded and eventually contracted.

Paul Wright

Note on Counties used and key to headings:

This book locates the individual station sites within the Counties that existed prior to the Local Government Re-Organisation that took place on the 1st of April 1974. In actual fact the Counties and the Boundaries that were set in 1974 were for the purposes of creating administrative districts and the original historic Counties were never actually altered.

In recent years many of the 1974 County Council's have themselves been swept away confusing the situation even further. The Author felt that using the historic County names would be easier for the reader..

STATION NAME	Indicates station closed to passengers pre-nationalisation
STATION NAME	Indicates station closed to passengers post-nationalisation
STATION NAME	Indicates station closed to passengers post-privatisation

KENYON JUNCTION (1831)

Date opened	Line opened 15 September 1830, but station did not appear in timetables until 1 March 1831
Location	West side of private road overbridge, about 150 yards west of Broseley Lane bridge (B5207), Culcheth
Company on opening	Liverpool & Manchester Railway
Date closed to passengers	2 January 1961
Date closed completely	1 August 1963
Company on closing	British Railways (London Midland Region)
Present state	Demolished – a fence bisects part of the site
County	Lancashire
OS Grid Ref	SJ644965

Kenyon Junction was one of the original passenger stations on George Stephenson's 1830 Liverpool & Manchester Railway (L&M), the world's first railway to cater for passengers as one of its primary functions; it was also arguably the world's first intercity railway. When the line first opened on 15 September 1830 work was already under way on a line that would link the Bolton & Leigh Railway (B&L), which had opened in 1828, with the L&M at Kenyon. This link provided the world with its first main-line junction between independent railway companies. The B&L had also been engineered by George Stephenson and was in fact the North West's first public railway.

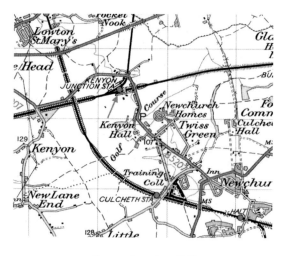

Kenyon Junction, 1953

Kenyon Junction first appeared in a timetable on 1 March 1831, and on 13 June services began to operate along the Bolton line. From this date the station was served by local trains running between the two major

Kenyon Junction: A view looking north-east along the Bolton line platforms in the mid-1960s. Although the station was in a remote location it had lengthy platforms and canopies, as it was at one time an important interchange point. *D. K. Jones*

cities and by connecting services running to and from Bolton. Over the years it developed into a substantial four-platform affair with buildings provided on each platform, the main buildings being situated on the Liverpool-bound platform of the 1830 line. Two straight platform faces served the Liverpool and Manchester line while two curved faces served the Bolton line. Effectively the Manchester-bound platform on the main line and the Liverpool-bound platform on the Bolton line formed a very wide island platform that narrowed as it got closer to the junction to the west of the station. The platforms were connected by a covered footbridge.

By 1864 the LNWR had taken over both lines and, with the construction of a line from the Bolton line a few miles north of Kenyon to Tyldesley via Leigh, a loop line was created, giving an alternative route from Manchester to Kenyon Junction. Passenger services started to use this route from 1 September 1864. Substantial goods facilities and sidings also developed around the station.

By the early 1900s Kenyon Junction had an extensive passenger train service and had become an important interchange point. It gained a reputation for being well-kept and often won the Liverpool District 'Best Kept Station' award.

On 1 January 1923 Kenyon Junction became part of the London Midland & Scottish Railway

Right: **Kenyon Junction:** A view looking east towards Kenyon Junction station in the mid-1960s. As can be seen, the station had four platforms. On the extreme right is the Liverpool and Manchester main line, and to the left the route to Bolton. *D. K. Jones*

Below: **Kenyon Junction:** The site of the station looking west in December 2005. This is the Liverpool and Manchester main line, which had opened to passenger services in September 1830. The flat area of ground in the middle of the picture to the right is where the Bolton line ran; it had a junction with the main line at a point adjacent to the signal in the distance. The station's main-line platforms were in the foreground. *Paul Wright*

Kenyon Junction: This view is looking south-west towards the site of the Bolton line platforms at Kenyon Junction in May 2006. The platforms that served the Bolton line were to the centre left of the picture on the flat ground. There were numerous goods sidings at this location, as indicated by the large expanse of flat ground. *Bevan Price*

(LMS). In the 1930s it was served by more than 70 trains per day on weekdays. Although mostly local in nature, some long-distance services travelling to locations such as Leeds and Llandudno also stopped here. Local services ran to Bolton Great Moor Street, Chester General, Liverpool Lime Street, Manchester (Exchange and Victoria), Earlestown, St Helens (Junction and Shaw Street) and Warrington Bank Quay.

On 1 January 1948 Kenyon Junction became part of the nationalised British Railways (London Midland Region). The station was located in a remote area of little population and over the years this did not change, its main role being to act as an interchange. On 27 March 1954 British Railways withdrew the Bolton Great Moor Street service, the last train on that line being the 10.35pm from Bolton.

With remaining eastbound services going to Manchester, either along the main line or via Leigh, there was little reason to change at Kenyon. On 2 January 1961 all passenger services were withdrawn, although goods services continued to use the station until 1 August 1963.

Interestingly, after closure many Liverpool to Manchester Exchange services continued to pass through the Bolton line platforms, using the Leigh loop instead of the more direct route along the original 1830 line. This situation did not last, however, as passenger services via Leigh ceased on 3 May 1969. The line closed completely shortly afterwards and was lifted, bringing an end to the historic junction. The station stood in a derelict state for some years after closure, but certainly by the 1970s it had been completely demolished and today there is nothing much to show it ever existed. The wide trackbed that accommodated the extensive sidings could still be seen in 2011, and the busy Liverpool to Manchester line was still very active, serving numerous goods and passenger services.

PRESTON BROOK (1837)

Date opened	4 July 1837
Location	South side of Chester Road.
Company on opening	Grand Junction Railway
Date closed to passengers	1 March 1948
Date closed completely	1 September 1958
Company on closing	British Railways (London Midland Region)
Present state	Demolished
County	Cheshire
OS Grid Ref	SD567806

Preston Brook station was situated on the Newton to Birmingham line of the Grand Junction Railway (GJR), which opened in its entirety on 4 July 1837. From 9 April 1838 the line connected with the London & Birmingham Railway (LBR) at Birmingham Curzon Street and became arguably Britain's first major trunk route. It would later become part of the West Coast Main Line.

Preston Brook station opened with the line in July 1837. The station was provided with two platforms situated in a shallow cutting on the south side of an overbridge, which carried the line under what later became Chester Road. On the northbound platform a single-storey brick building housed the station's booking facilities and a waiting room. Access to the northbound platform was via a sloping footpath that led up to the road.

On the southbound platform, which was reached by a set of steps, there was a simple waiting shelter, and to the east of it a station master's house was provided. There were no goods facilities adjacent to the actual station, but 200 metres to the south there were sidings and a goods shed adjacent to the Trent & Mersey Canal, just to the south of its junction with the Bridgewater Canal.

Although from the very start the line was a busy trunk route, Preston Brook station was served only by local services.

On 16 July 1846 Preston Brook became part of the

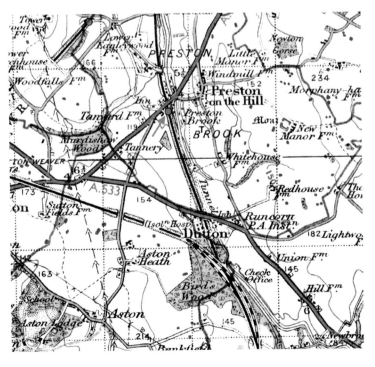

Preston Brook, 1949

Preston Brook: Looking north from the southbound platform at Preston Brook station in the early years of the 20th century. Although the line through the station was a major truck route between London and Glasgow, by this time the station was served only by local stopping trains. *Halton Borough Council Collection*

London & North Western Railway (LNWR), and remained very much a local station during the LNWR years. In 1923 the station became part of the LMS, and by the summer of 1932 it had ten northbound trains on weekdays; four went to St Helens, three to Newton le Willows, two to Earlestown and one to Preston. In the southbound direction there were also ten trains, five for Crewe, three for Over & Wharton and two for Acton Bridge.

From 1 January 1948 Preston Brook became part of British Railways (London Midland Region) and, being in a sparsely populated area, it was not profitable so BR closed it to passenger services on 1 March, although it continued to be used by

Preston Brook: The main facilities at Preston Brook were on the northbound platform. In this view from the early part of the 20th century the simple single-storey station building is clearly shown. *John Mann collection*

railwaymen until April 1952, and the goods yard remained in use until 1 September 1958. The station was demolished some time after this date, but the station master's house is still extant. The line through the station site is still in use and as busy as ever. It was electrified in the early 1970s and today sees a steady stream of express passenger services as well as a variety of freight.

Preston Brook: By June 1980 nothing remained to show that a station had ever existed here. *John Mann collection*

Preston Brook: The site of the station looking south in January 2011. *Paul Wright*

Preston Brook: Although nothing remained of the station at Preston Brook in January 2011, the original station master's house had survived as a private dwelling. *Paul Wright*

PENNINGTON (1846)

Date opened	Mid-1846
Location	Under A572 at south side of junction with A572, St Helens Road
Company on opening	London & North Western Railway
Date closed to passengers	29 March 1954
Date closed completely	29 March 1954
Company on closing	British Railways (London Midland Region)
Present state	Lost under the A579 Lowton Bypass
County	Lancashire
OS Grid Ref	SJ646985

Pennington: A view looking south from the St Helens Road at Pennington station in the early part of the 20th century. The station was very well kept by its staff and excelled with its floral decorations. *John Mann collection*

Pennington, 1953

Pennington station was on the Kenyon Junction to Bolton line, which had opened in stages from 1828 to 1831 as the Bolton & Leigh Railway, and was located on the south side of St Helens Road. The first section of the line from Bolton to Chequerbent opened on 28 August 1828. It had been engineered by George Stephenson, who was also working on the Liverpool & Manchester Railway, and it was one of Stephenson's locomotives, *Lancashire Witch*, that made the inaugural run on the line. The line had reached Leigh by March 1830, but it was not until 2 June 1831, when the line reached Kenyon Junction on the Liverpool & Manchester Railway, that passenger services began. The first passenger run was an excursion from Bolton to Newton for a horse-racing event.

Pennington: In March 1969 a diverted Trans-Pennine service heads south through the site of the station. It had been demolished by this date, and that year was to be the last of the line's operation. *Bevan Price*

Pennington Station opened as Bradshaw Leach in the summer months of 1846. By 16 July of that year the line had become part of the London & North western Railway (LNWR). Passenger services at Bradshaw Leach would have been mostly local trains running between Bolton and points along the LMR.

On 1 September 1864 the LNWR opened a new line from a point just to the north of the station to Tyldersley via Leigh. This provided the station with additional passenger business, and by this time it had developed into a two-

Pennington: Looking south on 24 April 1976 nothing remains of Pennington Station. It had been demolished some time after 1965 and the line was lifted in 1969. The trackbed would later be used for the route of the Lowton Bypass. *John Mann collection*

platform facility with a brick building on the Kenyon Junction platform and a simple waiting shelter on the Bolton/Tyldersley platform.

The LNWR renamed Bradshaw Leach station as Pennington on 1 February 1877. On 9 March 1885 a further line opened from the same point north of the station as the Tyldesley line, but this time went to Platt Bridge near Wigan, created a three-way junction. Pennington had a frequent passenger service to Bolton Great Moor Street, Manchester via Tyldesley and to Kenyon Junction and points west along the LMR.

On 3 October 1904 Buffalo Bill's famous 'Wild West Show' came to Pennington station, arriving in three trains and said to have included 400 horses and 800 artistes. The show itself was staged in fields close to the station.

On 1 January 1923 Pennington station became part of the LMS, and by the summer of 1932 it had 11 trains to Bolton Great Moor Street, three to Earlestown, eight to Kenyon Junction, 13 to Liverpool Lime Street, seven to Manchester Exchange, seven to Tyldesley, three to Warrington Bank Quay, and one to Leigh.

Passing to British Railways (London Midland Region) on nationalisation in 1948, by the 1950s services on the Great Moor Street route had declined to only six in each direction. On 27 March 1954 the passenger service between Kenyon Junction and Bolton Great Moor Street was withdrawn, and the intermediate stations along the route, including Pennington, were closed. Pennington station was demolished in the mid-1960s.

Pennington: In this view looking south at the site of the station in May 2006, the road running off into the distance follows the course of the railway towards Kenyon. The bridge that once carried the St Helens Road over the line has been replaced by a crossroads. *Bevan Price*

Passenger trains continued to pass through the station site going east at the junction to follow the line through Leigh to Tyldersley. Most services using this line operated on a service pattern of Liverpool to Manchester and beyond, rather than the main Liverpool to Manchester line via Glazebury. The line through Leigh became known as the Leigh Loop, as by this time it was effectively just that, a line that looped from Kenyon Junction to Eccles via Pennington, Leigh and Tyldersley. Goods services and excursions continued to use the line to the north of Pennington until 1963, when it was closed completely. The Platt Bridge line had already closed by that date. Passenger services through the site of the station ceased on 3 May 1969, the line was closed and lifted shortly afterwards.

The course of the line survived into the 1970s but was eventually used for the A579 Lowton Bypass. The St Helens Road, which had been carried over the line on a bridge, crosses the A579 on the level at a crossroads. Nothing remains of the station or the railway line that it served.

STUBBINS (1847)

Date opened	January 1847
Location	North side of Bolton Road North
Company on opening	East Lancashire Railway
Date closed to passengers	5 June 1972
Date closed completely	5 June 1972
Company on closing	British Rail (London Midland Region)
Present state	Both platforms and the station subway survive
County	Lancashire

Stubbins station was officially opened in January 1847, on the East Lancashire Railway (ELR) Clifton Junction to Rawtenstall line, which had opened to public services on 28 September 1846.

The idea for a line between Clifton Junction and Rawtenstall via Bury dated back to a meeting on 24 September 1843, the result of which was the creation of the Manchester, Bury & Rossendale Railway (MB&RR), which was formally incorporated on 4 July 1844. While the line was under construction the MB&RR amalgamated with the Blackburn, Bury, Accrington & Colne Extension Railway, and the new concern became the East Lancashire Railway on 21 July 1845.

At its opening the line through Stubbins was double track, so the station was provided with two platforms high up on an embankment. A bridge took Bolton Road North under the line to the south of the station site, and a booking office was provided at road level on the north side of the road, east of the line. The stone building had two storeys, the lower at road level and the upper at platform level; steps led up to the platform at the southern end of the building.

At the time of opening five passenger trains ran on weekdays in each direction between Manchester and Rawtenstall, with four trains on Sundays.

On 17 August 1848 the line through Stubbins became part of a secondary branch as from that date the ELR opened a line from Stubbins Junction, immediately south of the station, northwards to Accrington. This created a main line from Clifton Junction to Accrington, but no platforms were provided at Stubbins. The new main line ran to the west of the station, which required the northbound platform to be quite narrow and also shorter than the southbound one. A subway at the north end of the platforms linked them.

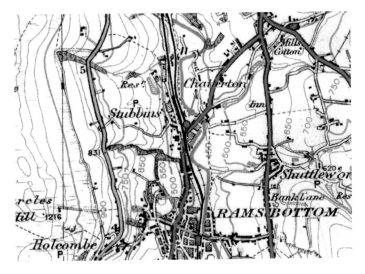

Stubbins, 1929

Stubbins: Looking north in 1962, a Colne to Manchester Victoria passenger service can be seen passing the station on the Accrington line. Within a few metres it will cross Stubbins Junction. Stubbins did not have platforms on the Accrington line – passengers wanting to travel northwards along that route had to first travel south and change trains at Ramsbottom. *Tony Harden collection*

The northbound platform had a fence at its rear to protect passengers from trains passing by on the main line. South of the station, on the east side of the line, a signal box was provided to control the junction.

In March 1848 the Stubbins to Rawtenstall line was extended northwards from Rawtenstall to Waterfoot, and four years later, from 1 October 1852, to Bacup. On 13 May 1859 Stubbins station became part of the Lancashire & Yorkshire Railway (LYR) when that company absorbed the ELR. During the early years of LYR ownership passenger services at Stubbins continued to run to Manchester via Clifton Junction, and later extensive goods facilities developed to the south of the station, including an area

Stubbins: In this view looking north in 1970, the line converging on the left is the up Accrington to Clifton Junction line and was out of use when the picture was taken; careful observation shows that a length of rail has been lifted to prevent its use, which was common practice at the time to indicate that a line was actually closed. The polished line in the centre is the former down Bacup line, but by this date it had become bi-directional and no longer went as far as Bacup. The line to the right, the up Bacup to Stubbins line, was taken out of use on 19 April 1970 and was lifted within a few months. *Tony Harden collection*

Stubbins: Looking north from the former southbound platform at Stubbins station on 27 May 1972, a two-car Class 105 Cravens DMU is standing at the former northbound platform, which by this date had become bi-directional, on a Bury to Rawtenstall service. The station had been reduced to a basic halt by this time. *W. A. Camwell*

Stubbins: Stubbins Junction was the point at which the routes for Accrington and Bacup diverged, and this view is looking north towards the station from the site of the junction in February 1983. The Accrington line had passed behind the platform on the left; Stubbins station never had platforms serving that route. The platform on the right served southbound trains travelling towards Bury until 19 April 1970, when the line became a single track and the northbound platform became bi-directional. When this picture was taken the line was out of use. *Nick Catford*

of marshalling yards.

From 1 September 1879 passenger services from Ewood Bridge towards Manchester followed a different route south of Bury, no longer travelling via Clifton Junction but on a new line via Prestwich.

In 1914 the LYR started a railmotor service between Ramsbottom and Bacup serving all local stations including Stubbins, and supplementing the trains that ran through to Manchester; the service was nicknamed 'Little Billie'. From 11 April 1916 through passenger services to Manchester were diverted to follow yet another route, via Heywood, which added a considerable mileage to the journey. The reason for the change was that from that date electric train services had been introduced on the Bury to Manchester via Prestwich line. Passengers

travelling to Manchester from Stubbins were encouraged to change to the electric trains at Bury for a quicker onward journey, and most of them did so. Within a few years many southbound services were terminating at Bury Bolton Street.

On 1 January 1923 Stubbins became part of the LMS, and the Summer 1932 timetable shows 20 weekday services travelling north to Bacup; the first, originating from Bury Bolton Street, left at 6.08am, a terminating service having arrived from Bury Bolton Street a little earlier at 5.45. The last service, which originated from Bury Bolton Street, left Stubbins for Bacup at 11.31pm. Only four of the 20 trains had originated from Manchester Victoria; most had started at Bury Bolton Street, one had commenced its journey at Bury Knowsley

Street, and one from Bolton. Some services started from Ramsbottom.

In the southbound direction there were 23 weekday departures, the first being a train for Middleton Junction at 5.41 am. The last train was for Bury Bolton Street, leaving Stubbins at 11.36pm. The rest of the services tended to travel to either Manchester Victoria or Bury Bolton Street, but there were trains at 9.21am, 10.41am and 3.16pm that went to Bury Knowsley Street, as well as shorter workings to Ramsbottom.

On 1 January 1948 Stubbins became part of British Railways (London Midland Region), and in 1954 the line between Bury and Bacup was considered to be busy enough to warrant the introduction of modern rolling stock, and it was reported in the local press that new diesel multiple units (DMUs) were to be introduced; they were brought into service on the line in February 1956. Stubbins had 35 trains in each direction, giving a half hourly service; this was to be the most intensive service that the line would see.

The purpose of *The Reshaping of British Railways* (the 'Beeching Report') of March 1963 was to create an economically viable network, involving the closure of many loss-making passenger lines and stations. The report's proposals for Lancashire and north Manchester were astonishing. The entire route from Manchester via Bury Bolton Street to Bacup and Accrington was earmarked for closure, yet the nearby Manchester-Oldham-Rochdale and Bolton-Bury Knowsley Street-Rochdale lines were not. The absurdity of withdrawing

passenger services on the heavily used, electrified service between Manchester and Bury was acknowledged when, on 8 February 1965, the Minister of Transport refused consent to closure. However, on 14 September 1966 the Minister gave permission for services on the Rawtenstall-Bacup and Bury-Accrington lines to be withdrawn, which they were on 5 December 1966, the final passenger train leaving Bacup on Saturday the 3rd. Stubbins ceased to be a junction and the signal box that controlled it was taken out of use at this date, although it was not officially closed until 17 April 1968 when the line through Stubbins became a single-track branch. The southbound line through the station was lifted, and the former northbound platform became bi-directional.

From 5 December 1966 the service through Stubbins became a shuttle between Bury

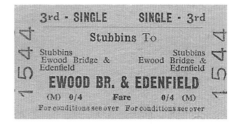

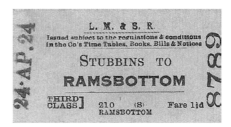

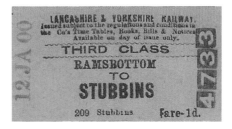

Stubbins: Looking south from the north end of Stubbins station on 13 December 2008, a Ramsbottom to Rawtenstall service operated by the preserved East Lancashire Railway passes through the closed station. *Mark Bartlett*

Bolton Street and Rawtenstall, and from 4 March 1968 all stations north of Bury became unmanned. The March 1967 timetable showed 15 services in each direction at irregular intervals, and two extra workings on Saturdays, one in the early afternoon and another late at night. No trains ran on Sundays. In the final year's timetable from May 1971 weekday services had been reduced to 12 in each direction, with 13 on Saturdays, the late-night Saturday working having ceased by May 1970.

On 5 June 1972 the service was withdrawn, and Stubbins station closed completely. The buildings were demolished but the platforms remained in situ. Freight trains serving a coal depot at Rawtenstall continued to pass through the station site until 1980. To mark the end of the coal trains a rail tour called the 'Rossendale Farewell' passed through Stubbins station on 14 February 1981, and after it had departed southwards the line was officially closed.

A preservation group named the East Lancashire Railway, after the original company, entered into negotiations with British Rail with a view to reopening the line from Bury to Rawtenstall. Supported by the local authorities, the group was successful and opened the stretch of line from Bury to Ramsbottom on 25 July 1987. At this time the former northbound platform was extended at its southern end across the site of the former Stubbins Junction, as the ELR considered reopening it. On 27 April 1991 the ELR opened the section of line to Rawtenstall, and once again trains started to pass through Stubbins; however, the plans to reopen the station were dropped and Stubbins remains closed.

Stubbins: On 14 February 1981 a rail tour, the 'Rossendale Farewell', passed through Stubbins station. In this view looking north, the rail tour can be seen heading towards Rawtenstall. Coal trains had ceased to operate along the line a few months earlier, leaving it with no traffic. After the rail tour was run the line was officially closed. *Mark Bartlett*

BURY Knowsley Street (1848)

Date opened	1 May 1848
Location	East side of Knowsley Street.
Company on opening	Lancashire & Yorkshire Railway
Date closed to passengers	5 October 1970
Date closed completely	5 October 1970
Company on closing	British Rail (London Midland Region)
Present state	Demolished
County	Lancashire
OS Grid Ref	SD804104

Bury Knowsley Street: A westbound passenger service arrives at the station in April 1951. To the left of the picture can be seen Knowsley Street's large goods warehouse, which was still carrying the name of the Lancashire & Yorkshire Railway nearly 30 years after that company had ceased to exist. *H. C. Casserley*

Bury Knowsley Street station was located on the Bolton to Castleton line of the Lancashire & Yorkshire Railway (LYR). The line had originally been proposed by the Liverpool & Bury Railway (LBR) as a means of creating a route to Liverpool. The LBR obtained an Act on 31 August 1845 allowing it to build a line from an end-on junction with the Manchester & Leeds Railway (M&LR) at Heywood to a junction with the Manchester & Bolton Railway a short distance to the south of Bolton. On 27 July 1846 the LBR was absorbed into the M&LR, and on 9 July 1847 that company became the Lancashire & Yorkshire Railway.

Bury Knowsley Street opened as plain Bury on 1 May 1848. It was situated on the southern edge of the town centre, a short distance from the site where Bury Market was held. It was on the east

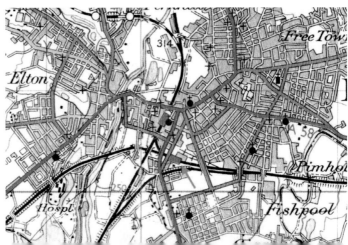

Bury Knowsley Street, 1953

Bury Knowsley Street: This view looking west from the end of the station on 25 June 1968 clearly illustrates the confined nature of the junction that was located to the west of the station. The line going off to the right led up to Bury Bolton Street station via Bury East Fork, which opened on 20 November 1848. In the centre of the picture a former LMS 8F locomotive hauls a train of vans up the steep gradient on its way east; the gradient was necessary as the line had just passed under the former East Lancashire Railway Clifton Junction to Accrington line. *Bevan Price*

Bury Knowsley Street: As can be seen in this view looking west along the eastbound platform at Bury Knowsley Street on 22 February 1971, the station had by now lost its canopies and had been closed to passenger services for four months. At the far end of the platform an English Electric Type 4 locomotive can be seen standing under the station footbridge; this was a replacement for an earlier structure that had collapsed under the weight of a football crowd on the 19 January 1952. *John Mann collection*

side of Knowsley Street, which passed over the line on a single-span arched bridge constructed of sandstone. The station was provided with a stone building in the classical style on the north side of the line. There were two low platforms, one adjacent to the building, which served eastbound trains, and an island platform that had two faces and served westbound trains. Goods facilities were also provided, located to the east of the station on the north side of the line. At the time of opening the station was served by trains running between Liverpool and points to the east of Rochdale.

From 20 November 1848 trains were able to run on to the East Lancashire Railway (ELR), which crossed the LYR

Above: **Bury Knowsley Street:** On 25 June 1968 a train of vans passes east through the station hauled by a former LMS 8F locomotive. At this time the station still had all of its features and looked very much like a busy principal station. In fact, the only passenger services that served it were the DMUs that ran between Bolton and Rochdale. *Bevan Price*

Below: **Aintree Central:** The north end of Platform 3 was the last to have track adjacent to it. In this view, looking south in the early 1980s, that section of track is seen here, a headshunt forming part of a siding. *Clive Hanley*

line at right-angles a short distance west of the station. A connection, known as the Bury East Fork, ran from the west end of the LYR station to the south end of the ELR's Bury station in Bolton Street.

On 13 May 1859 the ELR was taken over by the LYR, bringing both of Bury's stations under single ownership and leading to an increase in through trains between the two. From 1866 the LYR Bury station was often described as Bury Market Place, but from the late 1880s the name Bury Knowsley Street became the norm.

Bury Knowsley Street: The main entrance and booking office were located on the street after which the station was named, as seen here after closure on 22 February 1971. *John Mann collection*

By the 1880s the facilities at Knowsley Street had become inadequate, so the LYR made funds available to carry out alterations. The works were undertaken in a piecemeal fashion starting around 1886 when canopies were added. In 1893 further works were carried out, which included the raising and lengthening of the platforms. By the mid-1890s the station had been considerably altered from its original form, with four through lines served by two platforms; the two middle roads were used by through express trains and goods services. The eastbound platform on the north side of the line was the longer at 230 yards, and at its east end it had a bay. The original building was removed and new brick facilities were developed in its place; at street level a single-storey brick building was provided on the north side of the line, containing a booking office. On the eastbound platform there were waiting rooms, a ticket collector's cabin, toilets for both sexes and a W. H. Smith book stall. The westbound platform also had brick buildings

that housed waiting rooms. Both platforms were provided with extensive canopies. A footbridge located at the west end of the station crossed over the four tracks and provided a link between the platforms. Goods facilities were also improved, including a large goods

Bury Knowsley Street: In this view looking south across the site of the station on 14 February 1981, the former westbound platform was still in situ, and cutting right through the station site from left to right can be seen the Bury Interchange Railway, which opened on 17 March 1980. A Class 504 EMU can be seen heading south towards Manchester over the crossing installed when the interchange line opened to allow coal trains to travel between Castleton Junction and Rawtenstall. Having gone to great expense to install the crossing, BR ceased to operate the coal trains at the end of 1980, making it redundant. *Mark Bartlett*

warehouse located adjacent to the eastbound platform towards its eastern end.

In 1916 Bury Knowsley Street gained extra traffic when passenger train services between Bacup and Manchester were diverted to run via the station, using the Bury East Fork and running to Manchester via Heywood and Middleton. The reason for the alteration was that frequent electric services had been introduced between Bury Bolton Street and Manchester Victoria, offering a much quicker journey to Manchester than the service from Knowsley Street, so very few passengers opted to use the latter other than those who were travelling to intermediate stations on the Middleton route.

On 1 January 1922 Knowsley Street became part of the London & North Western Railway, but a year later that company was in turn absorbed into the London Midland & Scottish Railway (LMS). By the summer of 1932 the LMS was running 26 eastbound trains and 22 westbound trains from Bury Knowsley Street on weekdays. The first eastbound train was the 5.12am for Rochdale, and the last was also for Rochdale and departed at 10.49pm. Westbound the first train was at 5.19am and went to Wigan Wallgate. The last left Knowsley Street at 9.43pm and went to Liverpool Exchange. Other destinations served included Bacup, Bolton, Hull, Manchester Victoria and Southport.

On 1 January 1948 the station became part of British Railways (London Midland Region). On 19 January 1952 hundreds of passengers

used Knowsley Street to board special football trains to Blackburn in connection with a football match between Bury and Blackburn Rovers. Just after 4.38pm the footbridge collapsed under the weight of the unusually high numbers, crashing down onto the line, killing one person and injuring 173 – some 136 passengers had to be taken to Bury General Hospital. Thankfully, fast action by railway staff prevented any trains from running into the footbridge. The fire brigade, police and ambulances arrived on the scene between 4.45 and 5.00pm, and amazingly the line was cleared of debris by 6.30pm and trains were passing through the station at caution.

An enquiry blamed corrosion of straps that held the bridge to the supporting beams. The enquiry inspector was critical of the railway authorities as in his opinion the corrosion dated back many years and should have been spotted when the bridge had been repainted in 1949. The station was without a footbridge until 1953, during which time passengers had to cross the line by means of a barrow crossing.

During the 1950s BR introduced perhaps the best service that Knowsley Street had ever seen. Many cross-country services were run, and regular services also ran to Bolton, Liverpool, Manchester, Rochdale and Bacup.

In December 1966 the Bacup services ceased to run through Knowsley Street, as did other services, and by the late 1960s there was only a Bolton Trinity Street to Rochdale DMU service. Demolition work on the station's canopies was undertaken before closure, which

Bury Knowsley Street: By the time of this August 2010 view looking east at the station site, all traces of the station had been obliterated. The railway seen here reopened to regular passenger services between Bury and Heywood as part of the East Lancashire Railway heritage line on 25 July 2003. For the reopening the line had to be lifted above its original level so that it could cross the Metrolink tramway on a bridge, which can be seen in the centre background. The Metrolink line follows the route of the 1980 Bury Interchange line, which closed as a railway on 17 March 1991. *Paul Wright*

followed on 5 October 1970. The station itself was demolished the following year.

Goods services continued to run through the station, but following the closure of the line between Bolton and Bury they only ran between Castleton Junction and the former ELR route via the Bury East Fork. By the mid-1970s Knowsley Street had only a single track running through it, adjacent to the former westbound platform, used by coal trains serving a coal depot at Rawtenstall.

In 1980 Bury Knowsley Street station was cut in half by a new line that ran to a new facility called Bury Interchange, built to provide an integrated transport hub for Bury, which opened on 17 March 1980. Bury Bolton Street station closed on the same day. The new station created an interesting situation at the site of Knowsley Street, as the line crossed the remaining single track at right-angles on the level at about the mid point of the former station's platforms; the crossing was necessary because coal trains were still running to Rawtenstall. This situation did not last for long, however, as the coal trains ceased to run at the end of 1980.

On 14 February 1981 the 'Rossendale Farewell' rail tour passed through Knowsley Street on a trip to Rawtenstall. It was to be the last passenger service to pass through the station for two decades. In 1987 the nearby Bury Bolton Street station reopened as part of the East Lancashire Railway heritage line. This line was a great success, but in 1991 it lost its connection with the national rail network when the Bury Interchange to Manchester Victoria line was closed and converted into a tram route of the Manchester Metrolink. The only option available to the East Lancashire Railway was to reopen the line via the Bury East Fork to Heywood. However, the ELR could not cross the tramway that ran through the site of Knowsley Street station on the level. The problem was solved by the construction of a bridge that carried the line over the tramway and was opened in 1993, obliterating the remaining sections of the westbound platform. Regular passenger services run by the ELR began to operate through the site of Bury Knowsley Street station on 25 July 2003.

Bury Knowsley Street: Looking west, this is the bridge that carried Knowsley Street over the line at the western end of the station. The date stone bearing the year 1848 indicates when the line opened; it was clearly visible from the platforms during its early years, but following its rebuild in the 1890s it was hidden by the station's footbridge. *Paul Wright*

HALTON (1852)

Date opened	March 1852
Location	South side of Wood Lane at its junction with Halton Station Road
Company on opening	Birkenhead Joint (GWR & LNWR)
Date closed to passengers	7 July 1952
Date closed completely	3 February 1954
Company on closing	British Railways (London Midland Region)
Present state	Station building extant and in use as a private dwelling; Chester direction platform also extant
County	Cheshire
OS Grid Ref	SJ538794

Halton station was situated on the Warrington and Chester line of the Birkenhead, Lancashire & Cheshire Joint Railways (BLCJR), which opened on 31 October 1850, but did not open with the line. Following a serious railway accident in Sutton Tunnel on

30 April 1851 a report by Captain R. E. Laffan recommended that a station be opened at each end of the tunnel and that they be linked together by electric telegraph. Halton was the station provided at the southern end, and first appeared in the public timetable with the name Runcorn in March 1852.

The station was located on the south side of a road overbridge that carried Wood Lane over the line. The BLCJR was a double-track railway, so Halton was provided with two platforms. The station's main facilities were located in a two-storey brick building on the south-east side of the line on the Chester platform. The building was rendered to give a smooth finish, and provided booking and waiting facilities as well as incorporating a station master's house. The station platforms continued underneath the Wood Lane bridge. An approach road connected the main station building with the public highway and formed the main

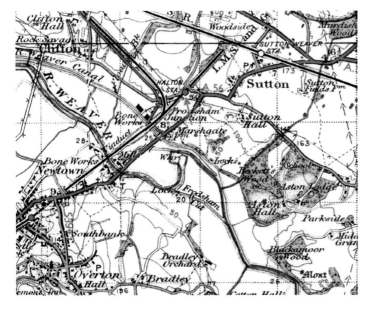

Halton, 1949

Above: **Halton:** Looking eastwards in 1967, apart from the absence of signs the station looks to be very much still in use, but had in fact closed 16 years earlier. By this time the main station building had become a private residence. *Halton Borough Council*

Below: **Halton** station is seen again looking eastwards in the 1970s. *John Mann collection*

approach to the station. Access to the Warrington platform was via a set of steps that led down from a gateway on the north-east side of the road overbridge. At the time of opening the station was served by trains running between Warrington and Chester and onward to Birkenhead.

On 1 August 1859 the BLCJR became the Birkenhead Railway, but within a matter of months it was taken over jointly by the Great Western Railway (GWR) and the London & North Western Railway (LNWR) as the Birkenhead Joint Railway on 1 January 1860. In April 1861 the new company renamed the station as Runcorn Road, then on 1 March 1869 it was renamed again, this time as Halton. The GWR used the line through Halton as a means of access to Manchester via Warrington and lines belonging to the LNWR. Halton station, however, remained very much a local facility.

In 1923 the LNWR share in the joint line passed to the LMS, which absorbed the former company as part of the 'Grouping' of the country's many railway companies into four large organisations. The GWR retained its own identity.

In the summer of 1932

Halton: The station building had undergone much alteration by August 2010, but it was still obvious what its original function had been and the line was still very busy with both passenger and freight services. At the time of closure the station had been in an isolated spot, but since the 1970s it has stood on the edge of a built-up residential area. During the later part of the 20th century consideration was given to reopening the station, but by 2011 no progress had been made. *Paul Wright*

Halton station was served by only seven trains in the westbound direction on weekdays. All of them went to Chester General, the first departure being at 7.41am and the last at 9.02pm. In the eastbound direction there were six trains, four to Warrington Bank Quay and two to Manchester Exchange. The first departure was for Warrington Bank Quay at 8:00am and the last was for Manchester Exchange at 7.35pm.

Halton station was in a fairly isolated location, so it was never very busy. It did not survive long after the nationalisation of Britain's railways in 1948, closing to passengers on 7 July 1952 and to goods on 3 February 1954.

The line through the station site is still in use today for goods and passenger services. The Chester platform survives and the building, although heavily altered, can still be seen, now in use as a private residence.

Halton: Looking south-west in August 2010, an Ellesmere Port to Fiddlers Ferry Power Station coal train approaches the station. Although at this time the former westbound platform was still in situ, nothing remained of the eastbound. *Paul Wright*

FARNWORTH & BOLD (1852)

Date opened	First appeared in timetable June 1852
Location	South side of Derby Road
Company on opening	St Helens Canal & Railway Company
Date closed to passengers	18 June 1951
Date closed completely	1 June 1964
Company on closing	British Railways (London Midland Region)
Present state	Demolished and lost under Watkinson Way
County	Lancashire
OS Grid Ref	SJ523879

Farnworth & Bold station was situated on the St Helens & Runcorn Gap Railway (SH&RGR), which ran from St Helens in the north to the banks of the Mersey at Widnes in the south. It was located less than half a mile to the east of Farnworth village.

The SH&RGR opened its line on 21 February 1833, and it was the company's intention that it would be purely for goods services, in particular the movement of coal from the St Helens area down to the banks of the Mersey, where the railway company had built Widnes Dock. Not long after opening the public lobbied the SH&RGR to provide a passenger service, so it hired two coaches from the Liverpool & Manchester Railway (LMR) at £1 per week in order to do so. It did not operate specific passenger trains, but merely attached the coaches to goods services. The only stations that were provided were at St Helens and close to Widnes Dock, the latter being named Runcorn Gap.

The passenger service was very slow due to the line being a single-track railway and because of two inclined planes up and down which trains had to be worked by means of a cable, being far too steep for locomotives to climb. One of the inclines was just to the south of the point where Farnworth & Bold station was later to be built. The other was at Sutton near St Helens.

Due to fierce competition with a canal, the Sankey Navigation, the SH&RGR was not a financial success. In order to overcome the problem, the railway and canal companies merged with effect from 21 July 1845 as the St Helens Canal & Railway Company (SHC&RC). This improved the financial situation and both the railway and the canal became profitable. The company then turned its attention to carrying out improvements. On 22 July 1847 it received Royal Assent to create a double-track railway and to level out the inclined planes so that locomotives could work along the entire length of the line.

The incline to the south of Farnworth

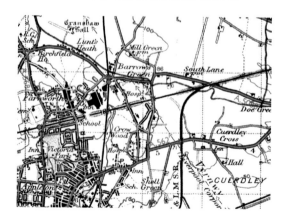

Farnworth & Bold, 1949

Above: **Farnworth & Bold:** An excursion train heads north through the closed station in 1958. It was laid on by Thomas Bolton & Sons Ltd to take its workers on the company's annual day trip to either a seaside resort or some country scenic spot, and started its journey at Widnes South station, close to the factory. The only clue that Farnworth & Bold station had closed by this date is the absence of station name boards. *Gordon Howarth*

Below: **Farnworth & Bold:** Following the withdrawal of passenger services in 1951 the Widnes and St Helens line continued to be used by diverted passenger services almost up to its closure. On 18 January 1976 a Class 108 DMU passes through the closed station with a diverted Liverpool to Preston service. *Bevan Price*

Farnworth & Bold: In 1978 cement empties depart for Widnes Hutchinson Street Yard. Class 08 locomotives operated trip workings between Hutchinson Street and Farnworth & Bold from the late 1960s through to the last months of 1981. *Halton Borough Council collection*

was levelled out and the new alignment was ready for traffic by the end of 1850. Shortly afterwards five intermediate stations opened along the line, all of which first appeared in the public timetable in June 1852.

Farnworth & Bold was known initially simply as Farnworth. It was situated on the north side of a level crossing that carried Derby Road across the line. It had a single-storey brick building on the northbound platform providing passenger facilities, with a simple waiting shelter on the southbound platform. There was also a signal box towards the southern end of the southbound platform. A crossing keeper's cottage was provided on the south side of Derby Road on the east side of the line, while goods sidings were provided on the west side of the line behind the northbound platform.

At the time of opening passenger trains operated between Runcorn Gap and St Helens. By July 1852 the SHC&RC had opened an extension of the line from Widnes to Garston, and this resulted in some of the passenger train services running on to the latter.

On 31 July 1864 Farnworth station became part of the London & North Western Railway (LNWR), which carried out further

improvements to the line, making it a very busy artery for freight. Factories sprung up along its route, including at Farnworth. By 1874 there was a manure works to the east of the station, and by the 1890s a brickworks had opened just to the west. Also by the 1870s a bridge had been constructed to the north of the station, and Derby Road was diverted to run over it; the level crossing was taken out of use, although the keeper's cottage survived.

On 2 January 1890 Farnworth station was renamed as Farnworth & Bold; this was probably to avoid confusion with a station that had been opened on the west side of Farnworth by the Cheshire Lines Committee (CLC) in 1873, which was named Farnworth.

By the early part of the 20th century large factories had developed just to the south of Farnworth & Bold on both sides of the line. A large wood yard had also developed on the north side of the Derby Road bridge. All of these facilities were served by rail and provided passengers for the station. Train services had settled into being very much of a local nature, although excursions were run to locations further afield.

From 1 November 1911 the LNWR

introduced a railmotor service on the line, and to coincide with its introduction it opened two halts, one of which was just over a mile north of Farnworth & Bold at Union Bank Farm. The service was very popular with local people and was given the name of the 'Ditton Dodger', as it ran between Ditton Junction and St Helens Shaw Street. At Ditton Junction connections could be made to Liverpool, Crewe, Manchester and even London. It was not long before the railmotor was inadequate for the service and it was replaced by Webb tank locomotives and coaches that could be operated as 'push and pull' sets. However, the name 'Ditton Dodger' stuck, and the service was referred to by this name until it ceased to run.

On 1 January 1923 the LMS took over, but very little changed and the service continued to run between Ditton Junction and St Helens Shaw Street. The LMS Summer timetable for 1932 shows 13 trains leaving Farnworth & Bold for St Helens and the same number for Ditton Junction on weekdays; additional trains ran on Saturdays.

During the Second World War the passenger service was cut back to only six trains per day in each direction, running only in the morning and evening peak hours. There were midday services on Saturdays for shoppers, but in the main the line was given over to goods services and troop trains. At the end of the war the services at Farnworth & Bold remained sparse, although the trains that did run were popular with local people for travelling to work and for Saturday shopping trips.

On 1 January 1948 Farnworth & Bold became part of the nationalised British Railways (London Midland Region), and the 1950 timetable shows morning trains to St Helens at 7.11 and at 8.15. There was then nothing to St Helens until 4.24pm, followed by trains at 5.15, 5.41 and 6.19. To Ditton Junction there were trains at 6.38, 7.03 and 8.40am, then 4.52, 5.36 and 6.12pm. As during the war, midday services ran on Saturdays. No services ran on Sundays.

BR wanted to concentrate on goods services so proposed the withdrawal of passenger services. Despite local protest and the fact that the replacement bus service took considerably longer, passenger services were withdrawn on 16 June 1951.

Farnworth & Bold: This view is looking north towards the station in the early months of 1981. Since 1973 the line to the right had been bi-directional following the singling of the line between Farnworth & Bold and Widnes No 1 signal box. A section of double track was retained at Farnworth & Bold to facilitate the movement of trains in and out of the Turners Asbestos Company's Everite works; the line on the left went into the works. *Paul Wright*

Above: **Farnworth & Bold:** Looking north in 1983, the station was in a derelict state. *Paul Wright*

Right: **Farnworth & Bold:** This is the station site looking south in December 2005. In the mid-1990s the site of the station was obliterated by the construction of the Widnes Eastern Relief Road, named Watkinson Way. *Paul Wright*

Farnworth & Bold station closed to goods services on 1 June 1964, although it was to remain on the railway map as a destination for goods trains that still served local factories. It is known that on 5 February 1966 a passenger service called at the station; this was an LCGB rail tour that was run to mark the end of 'push and pull' trains, and was booked to stop at Farnworth & Bold for 10 minutes to allow photographs to be taken.

In December 1967 the line from Widnes Junction to St Helens was reduced to goods line status, although interestingly diverted passenger services continued to use it right up until the early 1980s. From that date the signal box on the southbound platform at Farnworth & Bold was only open from 10.00 until 22.00 Monday to Saturday. With effect from 14 December 1969 the line was singled from a point to the north of the Derby Road bridge through to Sutton Oak. The signal box now took on an important role, as trains had to stop to collect or pick up the single-line token that was required for the Sutton Oak to Farnworth & Bold section. Because of this its opening hours were altered to 06.00 until the last train had passed, Monday to Saturday. The box also controlled the twice-daily 'trip' workings that operated from Widnes Hutchinson Street Yard to the Turners Asbestos Company factory adjacent to the station. The trip brought in Presflo cement wagons from Hope in Derbyshire, which carried tickets that stated 'Hope to Farnworth & Bold'. In the late 1960s one of these workings derailed as it was leaving the factory and the wagons fell against the former northbound platform of Farnworth & Bold station, causing damage to the southern end of it.

With effect from 4 November 1973 the section of line from Farnworth & Bold to

Widnes No 1 signal box was singled, and Farnworth & Bold box closed. At the station site a section of double track was retained from a point several hundred metres to the south of the site to a point several hundred metres to the north of the Derby Road bridge; the line adjacent to the northbound platform was effectively now a run-round loop for the Turners trains, while the line adjacent to the southbound platform became a bi-directional single track.

Until Farnworth & Bold signal box closed the station had remained in relatively good repair, but after 1973 its platforms began to become choked with vegetation. The station building had remained in use after its closure in 1964 for a variety of industrial purposes unrelated to the railway. Towards the end of the 1970s it had become the offices of the Roy Jacks removal company. When the Turners Asbestos Company announced that it was no longer going to be using the railway to bring in materials, BR decided that it could close the line as a through route and divert through trains. It announced its intention in 1981, and as it had been 30 years since passenger services had run the decision caused no protest. The line closed as a through route on 1 November 1981 but the last trains had operated a few days earlier.

Farnworth & Bold's station building was burned down just before the line closed, and the line was severed at the station almost immediately. At first the track was lifted northwards to Clock Face, then early in 1982 it was lifted south for about a mile.

The station site survived until the mid-1990s, when it was swallowed up under a new bypass that became Watkinson Way. Today there is no sign that the station ever existed.

RAINFORD VILLAGE (1858)

Date opened	1 February 1858
Location	North side of B5205 in Rainford village
Company on opening	St Helens Canal & Railway Company
Date closed to passengers	16 June 1951
Date closed completely	6 July 1964
Company on closing	British Railways (London Midland Region)
Present state	Demolished
County	Lancashire
OS Grid Ref	SD478010

Rainford Village station was on part of a railway route that linked St Helens with Ormskirk via Rainford. The route was effectively made up of two different lines that opened within a month of each other. The station was situated on the St Helens to Rainford Junction line, which was opened by the St Helens Canal & Railway Company (SHC&RC) on 1 February 1858. The other part of the line ran from Rainford Junction to Ormskirk, and was opened by the East Lancashire Railway (ELR). Rainford Junction itself was located on the main line of the Lancashire & Yorkshire Railway (LYR) between Liverpool and Wigan.

Rainford Village station opened with the line as Rainford. Other stations were provided at St Helens (third), Gerards Bridge, Moss Bank and Rainford Junction. A few months later the railway company decided to add another two experimental stops to see if they were viable; one of these was at Crank, the other at Rookery.

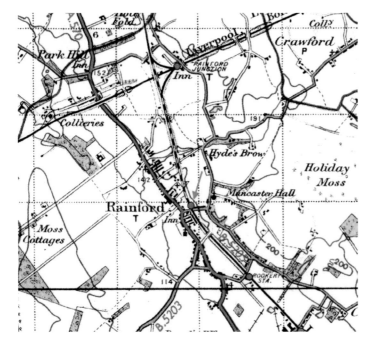

The station was located in a good central location in its village namesake on the north side of a level crossing that carried what would become the B5205 across the line. The line was double track through the station, which was provided with two platforms. The booking office was located in a timber building on the northbound platform, while a simple wooden shelter was provided for passengers travelling in the St Helens direction.

Rainford Village, 1949

Above: **Rainford Village:** As can be seen in this view looking south in the late 1940s, the station had only basic timber-built facilities. The station sign on the left dates from the LMS period. *Tony Harden collection*

Below: **Rainford Village:** The track was lifted shortly after the last goods trains ran in 1964, and this is the view looking north along the northbound platform in 1968. *Tony Graham*

At the time of opening Rainford station was served by four trains each way per day, which ran between St Helens and Rainford Junction, where the SHC&RC had its own platform. Passengers wanting to travel onward to Ormskirk had to change at Rainford Junction to ELR services, as no through trains were provided.

In 1861 the station was renamed as Rainford Village, but interestingly it was still being referred to simply as Rainford in timetables until 1864. On 4 August 1864 the St Helens and Rainford Junction line became part of the London & North Western Railway (LNWR), which was by 1904 operating eight trains in each direction from Rainford Village.

On 1 October 1911 the LNWR introduced a railmotor

service onto the line, which became known as 'The Flying Flea'. The railmotor was replaced after only a few years by tank locomotives and coaches that could operate in 'push and pull' mode.

On 1 January 1923 the St Helens to Rainford Junction line became part of the LMS. The Rainford Junction to Ormskirk line, which had become part of the Lancashire & Yorkshire Railway, also became part of the LMS, but despite this through passenger services from Rainford Village to Ormskirk were still not introduced and passengers still had to change trains at Rainford Junction.

By the summer of 1932 Rainford Village had 15 trains to St Helens and 16 to Rainford Junction. The first St Helens service left at 7.00am and the last at 10.19pm. The first service for Rainford Junction was at 6.42am and the last left Rainford Village at 10.58pm. Most of the services had good onward connections to Ormskirk, although some gave passengers only 2 minutes to cross over to the Ormskirk platform at Rainford Junction.

During the Second World War passenger services were reduced so that the line could be given over to a more intense goods service. At the end of the war service levels remained poor, and competition from a more frequent bus service led to many local people deserting the railway.

On 1 January 1948 the railways were nationalised, and by this time only three workmen's trains operated during the morning and afternoon rush hour in each direction. Despite protests, regular passenger services ceased on 16 June 1951, although the line through Rainford Village station remained in use for goods services and for passenger excursions and diversions until 6 July 1964. The platforms remained extant into the 1970s, after which the site of the station was developed with housing.

Rainford Village: In the 1970s the station site was lost under a housing development. In this picture looking north in February 2006 the photographer is standing on what would have been the trackbed of the line to the south of the level crossing, and the station was on the far side of the road that runs from left to right. *Bevan Price*

SKELMERSDALE (1858)

Date opened	1 March 1858
Location	Junction of Ormskirk Road, Neverstitch Road and Railway Road
Company on opening	East Lancashire Railway
Date closed to passengers	5 November 1956
Date closed completely	4 November 1963
Company on closing	British Railways (London Midland Region)
Present state	Demolished; site and trackbed occupied by B5312 Railway Road
County	Lancashire
OS Grid Ref	SD464063

Skelmersdale station was situated on the Ormskirk and Rainford Junction line of the East Lancashire Railway (ELR). The line made an end-on connection with the St Helens and Rainford Junction line of the St Helens Canal & Railway Company (SHC&RC), and had an north-to-east connection with the Liverpool and Wigan line of the Lancashire &

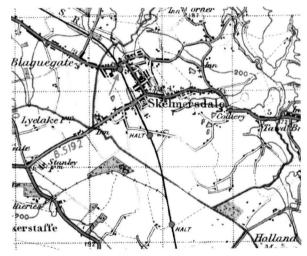

Skelmersdale, 1949

Skelmersdale: In this view looking north in the early part of the 20th century the station's goods facilities can be seen on the right. *John Alsop collection*

Yorkshire Railway (LYR).

Skelmersdale station opened as Blague Gate on 1 March 1858, located on the south side of a level crossing that carried the Ormskirk Road over the line. The line was double track so the station was provided with two platforms with brick-built booking facilities on the northbound (Ormskirk) platform. For southbound (Rainford Junction) passengers a wooden shelter was provided. At the station's north end on the east side of the line there was a signal box that controlled the crossing. The station was also provided with a footbridge adjacent to the crossing.

From its opening, Blague Gate was served by trains running between Ormskirk and Rainford Junction. There were four trains in each direction, but none ran through to St Helens; passengers wishing to travel onward to St Helens had to change trains at Rainford Junction.

On 13 May 1859 the ELR was taken over by the LYR, and by 1864 the SHC&RC was part of the London & North Western Railway (LNWR). On 1 August 1874 the LYR renamed Blague Gate station as Skelmersdale.

In 1906 the LYR introduced a railmotor onto the line. This proved so popular that the

LYR opened three halts, two to the south of Skelmersdale station at White Moss, opened in 1907, and Heys, opened in 1911, and one to the north at Westhead, which also opened in 1907. The railmotor provided Skelmersdale station with 19 services in each direction on weekdays.

On 1 January 1922 the LYR merged with the LNWR, which brought the entire line from Ormskirk to St Helens under the ownership of one company for the first time. Through passenger services, however, were still not introduced. One year later the LNWR became part of the London Midland & Scottish Railway (LMS).

The LMS replaced the railmotor with a 'push and pull' locomotive and coaches, and in the summer of 1932 Skelmersdale was provided with 17 services to Rainford Junction and 18 to Ormskirk on weekdays. The first Ormskirk departure was at 7.03am and the last at 11.13pm, while the first departure for Rainford Junction was at 6.45am and the last at 10.43pm.

Skelmersdale: A postcard view of the station, also from the early 20th century. The picture gives a good illustration of the passenger facilities that were provided here. *John Alsop collection*

During the Second World War there was a reduction in services, and after the war Skelmersdale never recovered the passenger numbers that it had lost. On 1 January 1948 the station became part of British Railways (London Midland Region), and on 16 June 1951 BR withdrew the Rainford Junction-St Helens passenger service; it also closed the halts on the Ormskirk line.

Skelmersdale continued to be served by passenger trains to Ormskirk and Rainford Junction until 5 November 1956, and by goods services until 4 November 1963. The line lingered on for goods services until 1964 and was lifted shortly thereafter. The station was demolished and the route of the line was lost under a road that was aptly named Railway Road.

Below: **Skelmersdale:** In this third view looking north along the southbound platform in the early 1900s a goods train can be seen standing adjacent to the northbound platform. In all likelihood it would have been collecting wagons from sidings as part of a trip working. *John Mann collection*

Bottom: **Skelmersdale:** A view looking south towards the site of the station in February 2006 – it was located to the left of the pub. *Bevan Price*

OLDHAM Clegg Street (1861)

Date opened	26 August 1861
Location	Both sides of Clegg Street, with the street-level entrance on the north-east side.
Company on opening	Oldham, Ashton-under-Lyne & Guide Bridge Junction Railway
Date closed to passengers	4 May 1959
Date closed completely	19 January 1968
Company on closing	British Railways (London Midland Region)
Present state	Demolished
County	Lancashire
OS Grid Ref	SD929046

Oldham Clegg Street was located on the Oldham, Ashton-under-Lyne & Guide Bridge Junction Railway (OA&GBJR) which connected Guide Bridge with Oldham via Ashton. Guide Bridge was on the Manchester, Sheffield & Lincolnshire Railway (MSLR), which linked Manchester and Sheffield, and was opened in stages from 1841. A link to Oldham was desirable and in 1857 the MSLR and the London & North Western Railway (LNWR) proposed a joint line that was to be constructed by a company that became the OA&GBJR.

The OA&GBJR line opened to passenger services to a temporary station at Oldham Mumps on 31 July 1861. The LNWR's station at Mumps had opened on 5 July 1856 and was on a branch line that connected to the LNWR Manchester and Leeds line

Oldham Clegg Street, 1953

at Greenfield. On 30 June 1862 the LNWR absorbed the OA&GBJR.

Oldham Clegg Street station opened on 26 August 1861, and goods services did not start to operate until 1 February 1863. The station was located in a cutting just south of Oldham Central station, which was on the Middleton

to Oldham line of the Lancashire & Yorkshire Railway (LYR). Central had opened on 1 November 1847. With the opening of Clegg Street the LNWR closed its Oldham Mumps station.

At the time of opening Clegg Street had seven weekday services to Manchester London Road and seven return journeys. The service was operated by the MSLR. From 1869 the

Above: **Oldham Clegg Street:** Looking north-east from the southbound platform at Oldham Clegg Street on 23 October 1954, a passenger train that probably originated at Guide Bridge waits to depart for Delph. *John Mann collection*

Below: **Oldham Clegg Street:** The southern end of the station is seen in September 1955. The picture clearly illustrates the layout of the station at its southern end. In the Delph direction there are two lines served by the island platform, while in the Ashton direction (on the right) there is only one through platform and a bay. *John Mann collection*

Right: **Oldham Clegg Street:**
In May 1959, on the last day that regular passenger trains served Oldham Clegg Street, this train carries a headboard indicating the significance of the day. The photograph was taken at the north-east end of Clegg Street station. The platform on the extreme right was not part of Clegg Street station, but belonged to Oldham Central station, which closed in 1964. *Bevan Price*

Below: **Oldham Clegg Street:**
This is the site of the station looking north-east on 20 July 1982. At this time a single track still passed through the station site but had been out of use for many years. *John Mann collection*

LNWR also provided services to Oldham Clegg Street, which included a through service from Rochdale to London Euston. Local services also ran eastwards to Greenfield and to Delph as well as along the original OA&GBJR to Marple, Glossop, Macclesfield and Stockport.

In 1900 Clegg Street station was substantially rebuilt, with a single-storey brick building at street level that contained booking facilities and office accommodation. It also housed a goods lift down to the platforms. The station had three through platforms that were built on a curve and extended on both sides of

Clegg Street; two of the faces were on an island platform, which served eastbound trains. The platform that served Guide Bridge trains had a bay at its south-western end; it also had a water tower that was capable of serving the bay and the through line to Guide Bridge. All of the platforms were provided with canopies. With this rebuild Clegg Street had developed into Oldham's largest station.

By 1922 Oldham Clegg Street was mostly used by local services. The LNWR operated a service to Manchester London Road via Guide Bridge and the Great Central Railway (to which the MSLR had changed its name in 1897) operated services between Stockport and Oldham, some of which continued on to Rochdale. Trains also continued to run to Greenfield and Delph.

On 1 January 1923 the LNWR became part of the LMS and the Great Central part of the London & North Eastern Railway (LNER). Being an LNWR station, Oldham Clegg Street therefore became part of the LMS, but the LNER continued to serve it. In the 1930s there were regular LMS trains to Delph, Greenfield,

Stockport and Manchester London Road. The LMS also had a service to London Euston. The LNER provided a regular service to Guide Bridge and ran some services to Rochdale. Interestingly the LMS also ran through services to Rochdale.

On 1 January 1948 Oldham Clegg Street became part of the nationalised British Railways (London Midland Region). On 30 April 1955 BR withdrew the service that ran eastwards to Greenfield and Delph, the last train being the 11.10pm to Delph. Services continued to run to Guide Bridge and to Stockport, but by this date Oldham Clegg Street had become very run-down.

Four years later, on 4 May 1959, Oldham Clegg Street closed completely to passengers, but remained open for goods until 19 January 1968. The line through to Greenfield saw its last goods train on 10 April 1964 and the route to Ashton closed in 1967. After closure to goods services, Clegg Street station was demolished, but a single track remained in situ through the site into the 1980s. Later the station site was developed with industrial units, and nothing survived of the station by the 21st century.

Oldham Clegg Street: Looking south-west at the station site in August 2010, it has become lost under an industrial development. *Paul Wright*

ROYTON JUNCTION (1864)

Date opened	1 July 1864
Location	About a quarter of a mile from B6194 Shaw Road
Company on opening	Lancashire & Yorkshire Railway
Date closed to passengers	8 May 1987
Date closed completely	8 May 1987
Company on closing	British Rail
Present state	Demolished
County	Lancashire
OS Grid Ref	SD934065

Royton Junction station was situated on the 6-mile 54-chain Oldham Mumps to Rochdale line, which was authorised by an Act of 1859 and built by the Lancashire & Yorkshire Railway (LYR). The Act also authorised a mile-long branch from the Oldham and Rochdale line to the town of Royton itself, which left the Rochdale line at Royton Junction. The line to Rochdale opened to goods traffic on 12 August 1863 and to passengers on 2 November; the Royton branch opened on 21 March 1864.

The station opened as Royton Junction on 1 July 1864 and was built by Patrick Farrell, who had been awarded the contract on 3 September 1862. It had four platform faces, two on the Rochdale line, numbered 1 and 2, and two more on the Royton branch, numbered 3 and 4. The Royton branch and the Rochdale line forked at the station, which gave a triangular shape to the middle platform (numbers 2 and 3). From platform 1 passengers could travel towards Manchester from the Rochdale direction, while from platform 2 trains travelled towards Rochdale. Platform 3 was served by Manchester-bound Royton branch trains, and platform 4 was for trains to Royton.

There was a single-storey brick building on the down Royton line platform (towards Royton), while the main station building and offices stood on what was effectively an island platform between the branch up platform and the Rochdale line down platform, with a waiting room provided on the Rochdale line up platform. Initially there was no footbridge; passengers were expected to cross the lines between one platform and another. A

Royton Junction, 1953

signal box that controlled the junction stood at the south end of the main-line down platform. To the north of the station, Royton Junction Sidings signal box controlled extensive sidings on the east side. The station itself did not handle goods traffic, although a private siding served the Windsor cotton mill to the west.

At the time of opening Royton Junction was served by 24 trains in each direction running between Rochdale and Manchester Victoria or, in some cases, Middleton, where connections to Manchester Victoria could be made. An almost equal number of trains served the Royton branch.

The line from Middleton to Oldham Werneth had a very steep incline (the Werneth Incline) of 1 in 27, which until 1854 had been cable-worked. Various proposals had been put forward to create a direct line from Werneth to Manchester that avoided the incline, but it was not until the LYR obtained an Act in 1873 that anything was done. This Act authorised the LYR to build a line from Thorpes Bridge Junction, on the Manchester to Leeds line but closer to Manchester, to Oldham Werneth. A contract was let on 30 June 1875, and on 17 May 1880 the new line opened.

With the opening of the new line a route had been created from Thorpes Bridge to Rochdale via Werneth, which eventually became known as the 'Oldham Loop Line'. Trains serving Royton Junction continued to run between

Manchester Victoria and Rochdale, but most of them now travelled via the new line, totalling 15 in each direction; a few services continued to run via the Middleton route.

In 1884/5 the platforms at Royton Junction were linked by a footbridge at the south end of the station.

On 1 January 1922 Royton Junction station became part of the London & North Western Railway (LNWR) when that company took over the LYR. However, a year later the LNWR was in turn absorbed into the London Midland and Scottish Railway (LMS). By 1938 Royton Junction station was still being served by 15 local trains on the Manchester-Rochdale axis

L.M. & S.R. FOR CONDITIONS SEE NOTICES,
CHEAP SINGLE TICKET
Valid on day of issue only
072   ROYTON JUNCTION TO
MANCHESTER (VICTORIA)   072
[THIRD]
0L=88   2018 (CST)   FARE ~/9½ C
MANCHESTER (VICTORIA)

Royton Junction: The station nameboard in November 1970. *John Mann collection*

Royton Junction: In November 1972 a Manchester Victoria to Rochdale service departs. By this date the station had actually been renamed as Royton, but it still carried its original Royton Junction nameboard. *Bevan Price*

and 22 other services, many of them shuttles between Oldham Mumps and Royton.

On 1 January 1948 Royton Junction became part of British Railways (London Midland Region), and during the last year of fully steam-operated services in 1958 there were 18 trains in each direction running between Manchester and Rochdale using the Thorpes Bridge route, and three Saturdays-excepted trains called that originated from Middleton Junction and travelled onward to Rochdale.

In June 1958 BR introduced diesel multiple units (DMUs) on the Oldham Loop. A Cravens-built type of DMU (later known as Class 104), which had twin power cars, used the line as the type was easily able to cope with the steep gradients. The service pattern at Oldham Mumps was a train every 20 minutes to Manchester, via the Thorpes Bridge line, and northbound trains also every 20 minutes. The northbound service destinations alternated with a service to Rochdale every 40 minutes and a service to Royton at the same interval. Two Saturdays-excepted trains continued to call on their way to Rochdale from Middleton Junction, but there was no service in the other direction. In total there were 29 trains between Manchester and Rochdale and 25 between Manchester and

Royton Junction: A two-car Cravens DMU departs in November 1972 on its way to Manchester Victoria. The station was in a very run-down state at this time and did little to encourage local people to use the railway. *Bevan Price*

Royton; this was the highest-ever frequency of service enjoyed by Royton Junction.

September 1964 saw a decline in services calling at Royton Junction. The service between Manchester and Rochdale became irregular, with trains calling at Royton Junction about every 45 minutes in each direction. Trains between Royton and Manchester Victoria were reduced to seven on weekdays in each direction, eight on Saturdays, and there were none on Sundays. From 7 September 1964 no trains operated from Middleton Junction. In 1966 further changes took place, including the closure of the Royton branch on 18 April. The service pattern was altered so that trains ran between Manchester Victoria and Oldham Mumps, with fewer continuing onward to Rochdale.

By 1968 Royton Junction had only an hourly service in each direction, and the platforms on the Royton branch were taken out of use. On Sundays 23 and 30 June 1968 the section of footbridge that crossed the Royton branch was demolished as the line had been lifted and the bridge no longer served any purpose. By 1972 the station had lost its buildings, which were replaced with simple 'bus shelters', and the gas lamps, which were still in use in April 1974, soon gave way to electric lighting.

Royton Junction escaped the attention of the Beeching Report, although the British Railways Network for Development map of March 1967, published when Stanley Raymond was Chairman of the British Railways Board and Barbara Castle the Secretary of State for Transport, showed that Oldham Mumps to Rochdale would not form part of the 'basic railway network'. Subsequently a footnote in the May 1972 passenger timetable advised that the Secretary of State had given consent to the withdrawal of passenger services between Oldham Mumps and Rochdale. However, by this date the South East Lancashire North East Cheshire (SELNEC) Passenger Transport Executive (the Greater Manchester Passenger Transport Executive – GMPTE – from April 1974) had stepped in and agreed to fund the continuation of the service. On 8 May 1978 the station was renamed Royton to reflect the fact that it was no longer a junction.

From the introduction of the May 1979 timetable the trains that previously ran only as far as Oldham Mumps were extended to run further north to Shaw & Crompton. The service through Royton became a train every 30 minutes in each direction, but a number did not call. Daytime off-peak trains called only hourly at Royton.

Royton station was not ideally located for the local inhabitants, having been chosen because of the junction that had previously existed. Once there was no junction, and therefore no need to interchange between lines, the station lost many passengers. On 30 September 1985 a new station was opened half a mile south of Royton; called Derker, it was closer to areas of population. In the Summer 1986 timetable trains called either at Royton or 'Royton – Derker' (as the new station was shown), the vast majority serving the latter station, and none calling at Royton in off-peak times. On 8 May 1987 Royton station was closed, and demolished shortly afterwards.

The line through the site of Royton remained open, and in the mid-1990s the GMPTE was looking at extending its 1992-opened Metrolink tram system. One idea that had been considered as early as 1984 was to use the Oldham Loop as a means of extending tram services to Oldham and Rochdale. By the beginning of the 21st century plans had been drawn up, and a few years later funding was in place to carry out the required works; to enable them to go ahead the Oldham Loop closed on Saturday 3 October 2009.

Royton Junction: Looking south-west towards the site of the station in September 2009, the Rochdale line platforms were in the centre distance near the point where the line starts to curve to the left. *Bevan Price*

LEIGH (1864)

Date opened	1 September 1864
Location	North side of East Bond Street
Company on opening	London & North Western Railway
Date closed to passengers	5 May 1969
Date closed completely	5 May 1969
Company on closing	British Railways (London Midland Region)
Present state	Demolished.
County	Lancashire
OS Grid Ref	SD663003

Leigh station was located on the London & North Western Railway's (LNWR) Tyldesley to Pennington line, which was opened in 1864. The line was a branch from the Eccles to Wigan line, which opened at the same time. Leigh was the only passenger station on the line.

Leigh station opened with the line as Bedford Leigh on 1 September 1864. It was located on a steep embankment on the north side of East Bond Street and was reached by 43 steps. The booking office was at street level. As the line was double track the station was provided with two platforms, both of which were constructed of timber. A small timber waiting room was provided on each platform. To the north-east of the station there was a goods yard that included a goods shed. To the south-west the line was carried through Leigh on a brick viaduct.

At the time of opening Bedford Leigh station would have been served mostly by local train services running between Liverpool and Manchester or on shorter workings along the route. Numerous goods trains also operated along the route. By 1870 the station was being used by more than 46,000 passengers each year, and within the space of five years the figure nearly doubled.

In the later part of 1875 passenger facilities at Leigh were improved, including the creation of separate ladies' and gentlemen's waiting rooms. On 1 August 1876 the station was

Leigh, 1953

renamed as Leigh & Bedford.

There was regular complaint from the Leigh community about the facilities at Leigh & Bedford station, and as a result the LNWR spent £1,500 in 1891 on further improvements to the platform facilities. Not long after the work had been carried out a fire caused major damage to the station and once again local people called for better facilities. On 12 January 1893 members of the Leigh Local Board travelled to London Euston for a meeting with LNWR Directors. The board pressed the LNWR to make improvements. The company agreed to spend between £5,000 and £6,000 on the station and £2,000 on an approach road, subject to the Leigh Local Board providing the LNWR with additional land at no cost.

However, despite the meeting no progress was made; indeed, proposals for moving the station were put forward, but they eventually came to nothing. On 25 May 1895 a further fire broke out – many locals rushed to the scene and urged the fire-fighters to allow the station to burn to the ground so that the LNWR would be forced into providing something better. After further wrangling a plan for an improved station was eventually put before the Leigh District Council (successor to the Leigh Local Board) on 31 October 1895.

Work commenced on the new station on 26 March 1896, the works being carried out by Messrs Hinson Brothers of Stafford. The cost was £17,000 and the station was officially opened on Sunday 1 April 1898.

In its rebuilt form Leigh & Bedford station had an approach road that led up to track level from the junction of East Bond Street and Princess Street on the east side of the line. At the top of the approach road was a large brick-built booking office and a parcels office; this connected to the westbound platform, which was longer than the original, and a subway provided a link to the eastbound platform. Being on an embankment, both platforms were constructed from timber, and were provided with waiting facilities, toilets and staff accommodation, also of timber construction. Both platforms had generous canopies.

The new station was welcomed by

Leigh: Looking east along the eastbound platform in the late 1960s, the timber-built station is clearly shown. It was provided with lengthy platforms that seem somewhat extravagant for the two-car DMU standing at the westbound platform. Excursion trains of considerable length used the station from its earliest days right up until closure, and to cater for these the station needed long platforms. *Tony Harden collection*

local people. Train services continued to run to Liverpool and Manchester but also to locations such as Chester and Warrington. The station also had an express service to Manchester Exchange, which completed the journey in 22 minutes.

On 1 October 1903 a passenger service was introduced between Leigh & Bedford and Wigan North Western, via Plank Lane and Bickershaw Junction. The very first service departed from Leigh & Bedford station at 6.43am and had only one passenger on board.

On 1 January 1923 the LNWR was absorbed into the LMS,

Left: **Leigh:** In March 1969 a two-car Derby-built Class 104 DMU pulls into the station with a stopping service from Manchester Exchange to Liverpool Lime Street. Although the DMU is wearing the corporate blue livery that was introduced in the later half of the 1960s, the station retains its British Railways London Midland Region totem signs from the decade before. *Bevan Price*

Below: **Leigh:** The site of the station is seen looking east in September 2010. After closure the embankment on which the line was carried was removed, obliterating all trace of the station. The trees in the middle distance mark the course of the line. *Paul Wright*

and by the summer of 1932 Leigh & Bedford station was referred to simply as Leigh. It had 31 eastbound weekday trains, most of them to Manchester Exchange but many terminated at Tyldesley. Some of the services originated at Leigh. The first eastbound service was at 5.10am and went to Tyldesley; the last was at 11.18pm and also went only as far as Tyldesley. Going west there were 23 services. Most went to Liverpool Lime Street but there were also services to Blackpool, Warrington, Wigan North Western, Kenyon

Junction and North Wales. The first westbound service was at 6.28am, which went to Kenyon Junction. The last was at 10.46pm and also went to Kenyon Junction. During the 1930s Leigh was still also served by numerous excursion trains that ran to seaside resorts during the holiday period.

On 4 May 1942 the Leigh to Wigan North Western service was cut, although excursion trains continued to use the direct route to Wigan.

With nationalisation on 1 January 1948 Leigh station became part of the London

Midland Region of British Railways. The station continued to be well served by passenger trains into the 1950s. In 1956 Leigh had a regular service to Manchester Exchange as well as through trains that ran between Manchester Exchange and Liverpool Lime Street. On Sundays some main-line services such as the Leeds City to Liverpool Lime Street train called at Leigh.

In the 1950s excursions were still popular. For example, on Saturday 5 July 1958 alone six excursion trains were run to cope with the holiday season. They ran to North Wales,

Leigh: Very little survives of the railway that once passed through Leigh. Just to the west of the station site a section of viaduct could still be seen in September 2010. *Paul Wright*

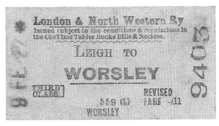

Fleetwood (for onward ferry to the Isle of Man) and Rhyl, and three went to Blackpool.

Service cut-backs began in the 1960s, although by the middle of that decade Leigh still had its Manchester Exchange service as well as its through trains between Manchester Exchange and Liverpool Lime Street. On 9 January 1967 the goods facilities at Leigh station closed, and the passenger station was also earmarked for closure. Despite this, many summer excursions still ran in 1967, 1968 and 1969, and on the very last day of passenger services, Saturday 3 May 1969, thousands of passengers travelled on excursion trains to

Blackpool. Local and long-distance services called at the station as normal, but after the last train departed it closed with effect from 5 May 1969.

Demolition of the station began in October 1969 and was completed by the end of the year. Track-lifting took place the following year, and the very last train to pass through Leigh station was a contractor's track-lifting train on 12 October 1970. The embankment on which the station had stood was also flattened. In 1985 the viaduct through the town was mostly demolished, leaving only a few short sections to show that there had ever been a railway at Leigh. The station site has since been developed for industrial use.

PLATT BRIDGE (1864)

Date opened	1 September 1864
Location	West side of A58 at Platt Bridge
Company on opening	London & North Western Railway
Date closed to passengers	1 May 1961
Date closed completely	1 May 1961
Company on closing	British Railways (London Midland Region)
Present state	Demolished
County	Lancashire
OS Grid Ref	SD604032

Platt Bridge station was situated on the Eccles to Wigan line of the London & North Western Railway (LNWR), which was opened in 1864 to provide a direct route between Wigan and Manchester that was able to compete with the Lancashire & Yorkshire Railway (LYR) line of 1848. The station opened with the line on 1 September 1864 and was located on the western side of the Platt Bridge to Westhoughton Road, the modern A58, over which the line passed on a bridge. The station was located on a steep embankment reached by steps that led up from the road. The line was double track and the station was provided with two platforms. At the eastern end of the station, close to the road overbridge, the platforms were constructed from timber, in all likelihood because the embankment narrowed as it got close to the bridge. Towards the west the embankment widened and the platforms were constructed from brick at that point. The main facilities were located in a single-storey timber building at the eastern end of the eastbound platform, which contained booking and waiting facilities as well as toilets. At the eastern end of the westbound platform there was a smaller single-storey timber building that provided waiting facilities. At the eastern end of the station there was a timber barrow crossing.

At the time of opening Platt Bridge station would have been served mostly by local train services running between Wigan and

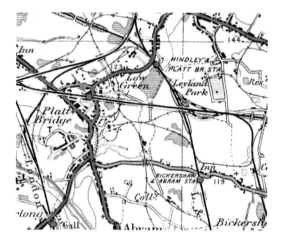

Platt Bridge, 1927

Manchester. The line became a busy trunk route for the LNWR, and numerous express services would also have passed through the station, together with a steady stream of goods trains.

In January 1922 the LNWR absorbed the LYR and a year later the LNWR became part of the LMS. This turn of events led to a decline in the fortunes of the line through Platt Bridge, as the LMS concentrated most of its express services onto the former LYR route. However, the line remained busy with goods trains and carried a number of excursions, and the local service continued to run. In the summer of

Platt Bridge: The station looking west. *Stations UK*

Platt Bridge: By November 1971 the line through the station had been singled, and no longer continued through to Eccles. This view is looking east along the site of the former westbound platform. At this time regular coal trains operated along the line carrying coal from Bickershaw Colliery. *John Mann collection*

1932 Platt Bridge saw 13 weekday trains to Wigan North Western, nine to Manchester Exchange and two to Tyldesley; extra trains ran on Saturdays. The first weekday departure was the 6.47am train to Wigan North Western and the last was the 10.45pm to Tyldesley.

On 1 January 1948 Platt Bridge station joined the nationalised British Railways (London Midland Region), and local services continued to serve it until 1 May 1961, when the station was closed completely, and demolished shortly thereafter. The Wigan North Western and Manchester Exchange passenger service continued to pass through until 2 November 1964.

The line closed as a through route on 6 January 1969, but the western end was retained and the line through Platt Bridge remained open as it served Bickershaw Colliery, to the south-east. The line was singled in the 1970s and trains continued to operate until mid-April 1992. The track was left in situ for a decade and was lifted in 2003. Nothing remained of the station in 2011 other than the trackbed of the former LNWR line.

Above: **Platt Bridge:** Looking east at the site of the station in January 2011. The station had been constructed from timber, so by this date there was little evidence to show it had ever existed. *Paul Wright*

Below: **Platt Bridge:** Looking west in February 2011. *Paul Wright*

WORSLEY (1864)

Date opened	1 September 1864
Location	South side of Worsley Road (A572)
Company on opening	London & North Western Railway
Date closed to passengers	5 May 1969
Date closed completely	5 May 1969
Company on closing	British Railways (London Midland Region)
Present state	Both platforms are extant
County	Lancashire
OS Grid Ref	SJ758006

Worsley station was situated on the Eccles to Wigan line of the London & North Western Railway (LNWR), which was opened in 1864 to provide a direct route between Wigan and Manchester that was able to compete with the Lancashire & Yorkshire Railway (LYR) line of 1848. The line also had a branch from Tyldesley to Pennington via Leigh, which provided a route to Liverpool.

Worsley station opened with the line on 1 September 1864 and was located on the southern side of Worsley Road, which passed over the line on a bridge. The line was double track and the station was provided with two platforms that were brick-built except at the southern end, where they were constructed from timber because at this point the line and station crossed over a steep-sided valley. The main facilities were located in a single-storey brick building located on the Manchester-bound platform, which contained booking and waiting facilities as well as toilets; it also had an awning that acted as a canopy over the platform. On the Wigan-bound platform there was a smaller brick building that provided waiting facilities.

At the time of opening Worsley station would have been served mostly by local train services running between Wigan and

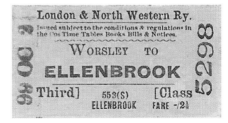

Worsley, 1953

Above: **Worsley:** Looking north along the northbound platform in the early part of the 20th century, it can be seen that the section of platform directly in front of the photographer was of timber construction but further along it was brick-built. The reason for this was because at its southern end the station was on a bridge. *John Mann collection*

Below: **Worsley:** In this early view looking south along the approach road, the main station building that housed the booking facilities can be seen in the centre. *John Mann collection*

Above: **Worsley:** Looking north in March 1975, by this time the line had been lifted but the brick-built sections of platform could still be seen. *John Mann collection*

Background **Worsley:** Looking south in May 2010, the trackbed of the line has been converted into a footpath and cycleway. *Mark Campion*

Manchester and between Liverpool and Manchester via Leigh. Being a busy trunk route, numerous express services would also have passed through the station, together with a steady stream of goods trains.

On 1 May 1875 the LNWR opened a line from Roe Green Junction, just north of Worsley, to Bolton. A service of passenger trains between Manchester and Bolton Great Moor Street was introduced, giving Worsley passengers further journey opportunities.

In January 1922 the LNWR absorbed the LYR and a year later the LNWR became part of the London Midland & Scottish Railway (LMS), which decided to concentrate most of its express services on the former LYR route. However, the Worsley line remained busy with goods trains, excursions and the local service. In the summer of 1932 Worsley station had 34 weekday northbound trains; 11 went to Bolton Great Moor Street, seven followed the route via Leigh, and the rest took the route to Wigan North Western. A few of the latter continued beyond Wigan to destinations such as Blackpool North and Windermere. The first northbound departure was the 6.18am to Wigan North Western, and the last was at 11.15pm, which also went to Wigan.

Going south there were 44 trains, all of which went to Manchester Exchange. Trains that had originated from Bolton Great Moor Street called at all stations to Manchester, while the Wigan and Leigh trains tended to skip many of the stations after Monton Green. The first weekday southbound departure was the 6.21am and the last was the 11.11pm.

On 1 January 1948, at nationalisation, Worsley station became part of British Railways (London Midland Region), and on 29 March 1954 BR withdrew the Manchester-Bolton passenger service; however, even by the summer of 1963 Worsley still had 22 weekday trains that ran south to Manchester Exchange, and there were 20 northbound services running to either Wigan North Western or Liverpool Lime Street. Trains operated on the line on Sundays, but did not call at Worsley.

On 2 November 1964 the service to Wigan ceased, leaving Worsley with services only to Liverpool Lime Street and Manchester Exchange. By 1968 there were 16 weekday trains to Manchester Exchange and 15 towards Liverpool, but some of them terminated at Leigh. The last goods services operating along the line to Wigan passed through Worsley station on 6 January 1969, and a few months later, on 5 May, passenger services were withdrawn and Worsley station closed completely. The line was lifted shortly

afterwards and the station buildings were demolished. The brick-built sections of platform survived closure, and when the route of the line was developed into a footpath they were preserved as a feature.

Worsley: In 2010 a section of the former southbound platform was restored and developed into a feature that also provided a seating area.
Mark Campion

STOCKPORT Tiviot Dale (1865)

Date opened	1 December 1865
Location	North side of M60
Company on opening	Cheshire Lines Committee
Date closed to passengers	2 January 1967
Date closed completely	2 January 1967
Company on closing	British Railways (London Midland Region)
Present state	Largely demolished in 1968, but a section of one platform survives, now heavily overgrown
County	Cheshire
OS Grid Ref	SJ896909

The station was opened by the Stockport, Timperley & Altrincham Junction Railway (ST&AJR) on 1 December 1865 as Stockport Teviot Dale. It was located on an extension of the Woodley to Stockport Portwood line of the Stockport & Woodley Junction Railway (S&WJR), which ran from Stockport Portwood to a junction with the Cheshire Midland Railway's Northwich Junction line at what became Skelton Junction. By 18 July 1865 both the ST&AJR and the S&WJR, together with a number of other small independent lines in the area, were formerly absorbed into the Cheshire Lines Committee (CLC). This was initially made up of the Manchester, Sheffield & Lincolnshire Railway (MSLR) and the Great Northern Railway (GNR). On 18 July 1866 the Midland Railway (MR) also joined the group as an equal partner.

Teviot Dale station was located on the east side of a main thoroughfare called Lancashire Hill, which lay close to the centre of Stockport. The main station building was on the south side of the line and was approached from a road that led down from Teviot Dale. The building was a large brick-built structure consisting of a two-storey centre with single-storey wings. A series of archways supported a canopy roof along the entire length of the building

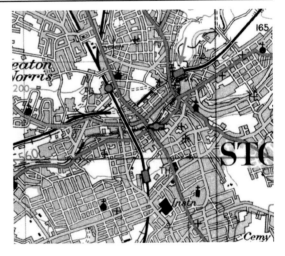

Stockport Tiviot Dale, 1953

adjacent to the approach road, giving shelter to passengers waiting for cabs or omnibuses.

There were two through platforms, and the main station building stood on the westbound platform, which was also provided with generous canopies that provided a good amount of shelter but also made the station seem a little gloomy. A covered footbridge to the eastbound platform passed over four tracks, two of which did not have platforms as they were provided for through trains. On

Stockport Tiviot Dale: This photograph by J. Clark shows a Manchester Central to Sheffield Midland Class 104 DMU waiting at the station's eastbound platform in 1964. *Manchester Local Studies*

Stockport Tiviot Dale: Another J. Clark photograph, looking east along the westbound platform on 30 November 1964, shows the very last stopping train to Liverpool Central preparing to depart westwards. It will take the direct route to Liverpool via Partington, although by the 1960s most services to Liverpool took the longer route via Manchester Central. *Manchester Local Studies*

the eastbound platform there was another substantial brick building and an extensive canopy.

At the west end of the station the line passed immediately into a tunnel, and the ramps of both of the through platforms extended right up to the tunnel mouth. On the eastbound platform adjacent to the tunnel was a signal box, Teviot Dale West. A bell was fixed to the tunnel wall next to the signal box, which was rung to let station staff know when a train was approaching.

At the eastern end of the westbound platform there were two bay platforms with an overall roof for terminating trains from the east. At the eastern end of the eastbound platform there was a single bay platform, so in all the station had five platform faces. An engine shed complete with turntable was located on the north side of the station.

At first train services were mostly of a local nature running eastbound towards Woodley and onwards via MSLR lines to the LNWR terminus at Manchester London Road, or westwards towards Northwich or even Liverpool via the route through Warrington Arpley. However, the CLC's constituent companies saw the strategic possibilities of the line through Stockport Tiviot Dale and in the late 1860s they obtained Acts that would have a significant impact on the station. On 1 August 1873 the CLC opened a line from Skelton Junction to Garston near Liverpool, giving it a main line from Liverpool to Woodley from where trains could travel onwards to the MSLR main line across the Pennines to Sheffield. On 15 February 1875 a spur was opened from Bredbury, to the east of Stockport, to Romiley, which gave a connection to the MR's main line to London via Matlock and Derby. On 1 April 1875 the MR started to run express train services between London St Pancras and Liverpool Central, and these stopped at Stockport Tiviot Dale.

From the start local people and the town officials referred to the station as Stockport Tiviot Dale rather than Teviot Dale, and in 1874 the CLC changed the station's name accordingly.

From the 1860s the LNWR had been hostile to the MR as it feared the competition of alternative routes, and made it increasingly difficult for the MR to operate express services into and out of Manchester London Road. The MR had aspirations to create a terminus station of its own in Manchester, and spotted an opportunity in 1873. An Act was granted to the Manchester South District Railway (MSDR) to build a line from Manchester to Heaton Mersey, to the west of Stockport. The MSDR struggled financially, so the MR took it over in 1877 and built the line connecting it to the CLC line at Heaton Mersey, which opened on 1 January 1880. The MR could now run train services directly into Manchester without relying on the LNWR. At first its trains ran into a temporary terminus at Manchester Central, but from 1 July 1880 they were able to use the new CLC Manchester Central station, which was arguably second only to London St Pancras in size and scale.

From 1880 Stockport Tiviot Dale station was served by long-distance express services running between the cities of Liverpool and Manchester to destinations such as Bristol, London, Nottingham and Hull. Other services ran to Chester, Warrington, Buxton, Derby and Sheffield. In addition, local commuter services operated at a high frequency to and from Manchester Central, while other local services ran eastwards to Woodley and Godley and onwards to Manchester London Road. Train services were provided by the three CLC constituent companies and by the CLC in its own right, although the latter never owned any locomotives of its own, using motive power provided by the MSLR (which became the Great Central Railway in 1897).

The situation at Stockport Tiviot Dale remained the same for more than 20 years. The desire for speed and the keen sense of competition between the MR and the LNWR led the MR to consider ways in which it could speed up its southbound express trains. The solution was to build a direct line between Heaton Mersey and New Mills at a cost of £2 million. The new line would cut out the need for trains to run via Stockport Tiviot Dale, thereby allowing fast express services to substantially improve journey times for trains running between London St Pancras and Manchester and Liverpool.

The new line was authorised in 1898 and work began immediately. Despite the need for some very heavy engineering, including the construction of a 2-mile-long tunnel at Disley, the line was ready for use by 1 July 1902. Because most express services would no longer pass through Tiviot Dale, a station was opened on the new line at Cheadle Heath, west of Stockport; thereafter most main-line services began to use Cheadle Heath, and Stockport Tiviot Dale lost its importance as a main-line station. Although it was still served by many trains, it would never again be anything other than a secondary station as far as main-line services were concerned.

During the early part of the 20th century passenger train services from Stockport Tiviot Dale operated to Buxton Midland, Derby, Liverpool Central, London St Pancras, London Marylebone, Manchester Central, Nottingham, Sheffield Midland and Southport Lord Street. The most intensive service was the local all-stations to Manchester Central, with trains running approximately every 20 minutes between Stockport and Manchester.

In 1923 the CLC remained as an independent company, but its constituent companies became part of the London Midland & Scottish Railway (LMS), which held a third share, and the London & North Eastern Railway (LNER), which held two-thirds of the shares. From this date the CLC train services were all hauled by LNER engines. During the 1920s and 1930s an extensive commuter service continued to operate to Manchester Central, but eastbound trains to Woodley declined dramatically. Many excursion trains ran from Tiviot Dale in this period, taking residents of Stockport to Chester, Southport, New Brighton (via the ferries at Liverpool), Buxton and the Peak District; indeed, in the 1930s ramblers' specials to the Peak District became very popular.

During the Second World War passenger services were cut back to allow more freight trains and troop trains to run. After the war things returned to normal, but the service to Woodley had been discontinued.

On 1 January 1948 the railways were nationalised, and Stockport Tiviot Dale became part of the London Midland Region of British Railways, and the CLC ceased to exist. During the 1950s competition from road transport began to take its toll. The overall roof over the bay platforms at the east end of the westbound platform was removed; passenger trains had ceased to use these platforms by the 1940s. By 1962 Stockport Tiviot Dale was left with one service per day to London St Pancras, a Liverpool Central to Nottingham express, only five local trains in each direction between

Above: **Stockport Tiviot Dale:** After the station closed the loops that had served the through platforms were removed, leaving only the through lines, which remained in use for goods services until 1980. This view looking east in February 1983 shows the through lines, and the platforms in a derelict state. *Nick Catford*

Below: **Stockport Tiviot Dale:** This April 2010 view is looking east along the bay platform that was located on the north side of the eastbound platform. By this date the through line platforms and trackbed had been buried under earth, but the bay platform edge survived in the undergrowth. *Paul Wright*

either Liverpool Central or Warrington Central and Tiviot Dale via Skelton Junction, five services to Sheffield, and five to Derby. A more regular service, but nothing like it had been in the past, continued to link Stockport with Manchester Central.

On 30 November 1964 the Liverpool Central/Warrington Central and Stockport Tiviot Dale service was withdrawn. In 1966 main-line services stopped operating from Liverpool Central, and Tiviot Dale lost its

Stockport Tiviot Dale: A view looking west along the former east-facing bay platform towards the buffer stops in April 2010. *Paul Wright*

Nottingham service. With only a handful of services left, the station closed completely on 2 January 1967.

As soon as the station closed the lines were removed from the platforms, leaving just the two former through lines to cater for the intensive goods service that still operated. In 1968 a demolition contractor, Messrs Dawson & Morris of Skipton, was appointed to remove the stations buildings and structures, and by 1969 only the platforms remained.

The line through Tiviot Dale was an important route for freight trains travelling between the Woodhead route and Liverpool, so it remained open throughout the 1970s and into the 1980s. One of the busiest freight services that continued to run were the coal trains that came from South Yorkshire and took coal to Fiddlers Ferry Power Station near Warrington. However, with the closure of the Woodhead route in 1981 the line lost most of its traffic. In 1980 works in connection with the construction of the M63 motorway (later to become the M60 ring road) damaged the tunnel that passed under Lancashire Hill, and the line was closed temporarily as a safety measure. By 1982 British Rail had come to the conclusion that as it had managed without the line for two years it could afford to close it. Consequently the section of line from Heaton Mersey to Bredbury, including the section running through Tiviot Dale, closed completely in 1982 and it was lifted in 1986.

The tunnel at Tiviot Dale has now been partially filled with earth and rubble and the station site is heavily overgrown, but sections of the platforms do still exist. There are plans to build a Metrolink tram line from Chorlton to Stockport using part of the trackbed.

NESTON SOUTH (1866)

Date opened	1 October 1866
Location	South side of Station Road; Station Close now lies on the station site
Company on opening	GWR & LNWR Joint
Date closed to passengers	17 September 1956
Date closed completely	7 May 1962
Company on closing	British Railways (London Midland Region)
Present state	Demolished
County	Cheshire
OS Grid Ref	SJ297773

Neston South station was opened as Neston on 1 October 1866 as part of the GWR & LNWR Joint Railway's Hooton to Parkgate branch line. Hooton was located on the joint companies' Birkenhead to Chester line, which had opened in 1840. At the time of opening three stations were provided on the line, the others being Hadlow Road and Parkgate.

Neston station was situated on the south side of the village of that name and was provided with a substantial brick building that incorporated a two-storey house for the station master. Facilities included a booking

office, a waiting room and a lamp room. Only a single track passed through the station, so only one platform was provided. Hadlow Road was a passing point, with two lines and two platforms. Neston was also provided with goods facilities, including sidings. At the time of opening passenger services mostly ran to and from Parkgate and Hooton, with some continuing beyond Hooton to Birkenhead Monks Ferry.

On 19 April 1886 the branch line was extended from Parkgate to West Kirby, after which the pattern of passenger services at Neston was westbound to West Kirby and eastbound to Hooton, with some going forward to Birkenhead Woodside.

In 1923 the line became GWR & LMS Joint, but things continued as they had done previously. In 1948 the line became part of British Railways (London Midland Region), and in 1950 nine trains operated in each direction on weekdays with four on a Saturday. Neston was renamed as Neston South on 15 September 1952 to distinguish it from the town's other station, which had opened in 1896. The Hooton to West Kirby line suffered from increasing road competition in the 1950s and its passenger service was withdrawn on 17 September 1956, when Neston South closed to

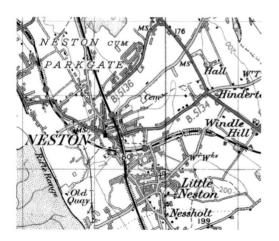

Neston South, 1952

Neston South. *Stations UK*

passengers. The last service to depart was to Hooton, having left West Kirby at 9.55pm.

In 1961 newly introduced DMUs passed through Hadlow Road station; however, they were not for the use of passengers, as the line was being used to train drivers in their use.

Neston South station continued to be used for goods until 7 May 1962. The very last goods train stopped there so that the train crew could remove any remaining fixtures and fittings that were of value. Early in 1964 the demolition gangs began their work and the line was lifted.

Neston South: In the years after closure the station is seen looking east from the west end of the single platform. Other than the nameboards it still retained its original features at this time. *Matt Doran*

In the early 1970s the route of the Hooton-West Kirby branch was chosen to create Britain's first country park, the Wirral Country Park. However, the site of Neston South station had been developed as part of a housing estate before the park was created, so nothing of it remains today.

Neston South: Looking east at the station site in August 2009, nothing had survived to show that a station had ever existed at this location. *Paul Wright*

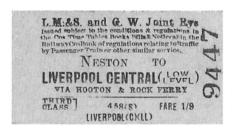

Neston South: This view is looking west along the former station approach road in August 2009. The road provided a direct link between the station and the centre of Neston. *Paul Wright*

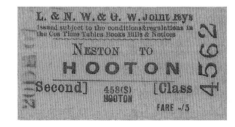

WIDNES SOUTH (1870)

Date opened	1 March 1870
Location	East side of Victoria Road
Company on opening	London & North Western Railway
Date closed to passengers	10 September 1962
Date closed completely	31 March 1969
Company on closing	British Railways (London Midland Region)
Present state	Booking office and westbound platform demolished; eastbound platform survives as do the access steps and other parts of the platform supports
County	Lancashire
OS Grid Ref	SJ513848

Widnes South station opened as Widnes on 1 March 1870, and was situated on the Widnes Deviation line, built by the London & North Western Railway (LNWR) as part of a £100,000 package of improvements designed to make traffic movements at Widnes flow more easily. The Deviation line, which opened to goods traffic on 1 April 1869, branched off the original Garston to Warrington line at a point slightly to the west of the 1852 Widnes station, and ran for just under 1.5 miles to the north of the original line before rejoining it at Carterhouse Bridge, which became known as Carterhouse Junction. The Deviation line passed over the 1833 St Helens & Runcorn Gap Railway, which ran between St Helens and Widnes on a bridge; the original Garston and Warrington line crossed the St Helens line on the level, causing much congestion. As well as passing over the St Helens line, the Deviation was provided with a spur connection to it, allowing the new station to serve both lines.

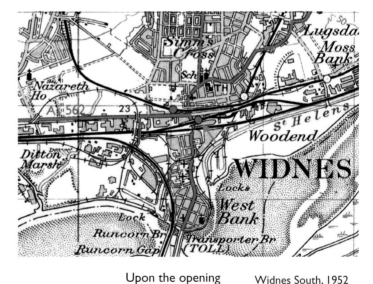

Widnes South, 1952

Upon the opening of the new Widnes station, the original station at Waterloo Crossing closed. The 1870 station was situated on an embankment on the east side of the bridge that carried the line over Victoria Road. A street-level single-storey brick building, situated on the south side of the line, provided staff accommodation, booking office and parcels office. Two platforms were provided; the westbound one was connected to the booking office by a set of steps, while the

Right: **Widnes South:** Joseph Robinson, a Widnes resident and a goods train guard for the LNWR, was a keen amateur photographer, and took this picture of Widnes station staff and a train crew in the early years of the 20th century. The picture was taken on the south side of the line at the foot of the embankment directly below the westbound platform. An access road led up to the platform on this side of the line, and can be seen in the bottom left-hand corner of the picture. *Mark Aldred collection*

Below: **Widnes South:** This staff photograph was taken on the eastbound platform looking east in the early 1900s. At that time the railway companies employed hundreds of thousands of workers, and as can be seen here Widnes station (it was not renamed as Widnes South until 1959) had what today would be considered a large complement of staff for a station of its size. This picture gives a good view of the platform buildings, which were situated on an embankment. In the background is Widnes No 7 signal box, which controlled the junction between the Ditton-Skelton Junction and Widnes-St Helens lines. A signal controlling trains coming off the St Helens line can be seen on the right. *Halton Borough Council collection*

eastbound one was reached by a set of steps from Victoria Road, and was also linked to the booking office by means of a subway.

Each platform had a single-storey timber building with canopy, which provided waiting facilities for passengers. There was also a shed on each platform used by station staff for storage. At the east end of the westbound platform there was a wooden signal box, Widnes No 7. This controlled the junction between the main line and the spur that ran down to the St Helens line.

When the original lines to Garston and Warrington had been built in 1852 and 1853 by the St Helens & Runcorn Gap Railway, which by 1845 had become the St Helens Canal & Railway, the intention was that it would become a main-line railway

connecting Liverpool and Manchester that would rival the LNWR's line connecting the two cities via Chat Moss. However, once the LNWR became the owner of the Garston and Warrington line it had other ideas. It decided that the Chat Moss route would remain as the premier main line and that the route through Widnes would be for freight and local passenger services.

At the time of opening Widnes station was served by trains that ran between Liverpool and Manchester and shorter workings along the route; some trains from Liverpool terminated at Widnes. St Helens line trains also served the station, running between Ditton Junction and St Helens.

Before a decade had passed Widnes station became subject to competition when a new joint line was opened by the Manchester, Sheffield & Lincolnshire Railway and the Midland Railway (MSLR/MR Joint), only a few hundred metres away to the north. A passenger station was provided on the western side of Victoria Road; known as Widnes Central, it opened on 1 August 1879. The MSLR/MR station was also served by trains running between Liverpool and Manchester, but by a different route.

In 1911 a railmotor service was introduced on the St Helens line, which became known

locally as the 'Ditton Dodger'. Twelve trains ran on weekdays in each direction and additional stations were opened. Local traffic running along the main line continued to be buoyant even with the competition from the nearby Widnes Central.

In 1923 Widnes station became part of the London Midland & Scottish Railway (LMS). Very little changed and passenger service patterns continued as they had done previously. In the summer of 1932 Widnes had 24 eastbound departures on weekdays; ten went to Manchester London Road, four to Warrington Bank Quay and ten to St Helens Shaw Street. The first eastbound departure was at 5.48am and it went to Manchester London Road. Thirty-one services went westbound, 15 to Liverpool Lime Street, some of them originating at Widnes, and 16 to Ditton Junction. The first westbound departure was the 6.10am to Liverpool Lime Street, and the last was also for Liverpool Lime Street at 10.23pm.

During the Second World War services on the St Helens line were reduced to only three trains in the morning peak and three in the afternoon on weekdays only. After the war the service remained at this level but some midday services for shoppers did run on Saturdays.

In 1948 Widnes station became part of British Railway (London Midland Region), as did Widnes Central, and the new nationalised railway company operated more Liverpool to

Widnes South: The booking office was located at street level on the south side of the line. In this view from 1959 the station signage would have been quite new as it was only renamed Widnes South on 5 January that year. Within three years it would be closed to passenger services. *Halton Borough Council collection*

Widnes South: Wearing the latest in early-1960s fashion, two young women purchase tickets from the booking office window. They could have been travelling to either Liverpool or Warrington for a shopping trip or maybe an evening out. The steps that led up to the Liverpool platform are clearly indicated by the sign. By this date though most Liverpool journeys required a change of train at Ditton Junction. *Gordon Howarth*

Manchester trains via Widnes Central than via Widnes. On 16 June 1951 the 'Ditton Dodger' service was withdrawn despite much local opposition. It had never been restored to its pre-war levels and no effort had been made to exploit potential connections with other services.

In the 1950s most of the services at Widnes station ran on a Ditton Junction to Manchester Oxford Road axis, with only a few connecting through to Liverpool, and some of the few Liverpool services that did operate only went as far as Warrington Bank Quay Low Level. At this time a Saturdays-only long-distance train, the 'York Mail', called at Widnes, giving local people a travel opportunity not usually available. Many special train services

Widnes South: Looking west in January 1982, a section of the westbound platform has recently been demolished to facilitate engineers who were engaged in the construction of a new spur a few hundred metres to the east of the station that provided a connection to the Tan House Lane sidings. The work also saw the demise in April 1982 of Widnes Junction, which lay at the east end of the station. The Tan House connection allowed the final section of the former St Helens & Runcorn Gap Railway at Widnes to close, thereby ending the need for the junction that served it. *John Mann collection*

also ran from Widnes in the 1950s, including works outings and Rugby League supporters' trains.

On 5 January 1959 Widnes station was renamed as Widnes South. At the same time Farnworth station on the former CLC main line a few miles to the north was renamed as Widnes North. For a brief period in the late 1950s diesel multiple units (DMUs) were introduced to the Ditton-Manchester Oxford Road service, but they were short-lived – by 1960 steam-hauled 'push and pull' sets, which had operated previously, were the norm.

On 10 September 1962 the Ditton-Manchester Oxford Road Service was withdrawn and Widnes South station closed to passengers. Widnes passengers could still

travel to Liverpool, Warrington and Manchester from the nearby Widnes Central station, which lasted until October 1964. The 'York Mail' continued to pass through until 1965, but did not stop. Rugby League specials operated from Widnes South until 1965, then the station closed completely on 31 March 1969.

Goods services continued to pass through the station after closure, as they still do today. The spur to the St Helens line, however, closed in April 1982, together with the last sections of that line in Widnes. Widnes No 7 signal box closed at the same time.

The platform buildings were demolished within a few years of closure, but the roadside building survived until the early 1990s, and for many years was used as a car repair garage. The eastbound platform was still very much intact in 2010, although somewhat overgrown. Only the west end of the westbound platform was still extant at this time, its eastern end having been demolished in the early 1980s.

Widnes South: Looking west along the eastbound platform in the summer of 1986, wild flowers have colonised the platform and provide a colourful spectacle. *Paul Wright*

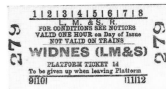

Widnes South: Looking east along the same platform in January 2005, at that time the line was mainly used by coal trains running between Liverpool Docks and Fiddlers Ferry Power Station. *Paul Wright*

HELSBY & ALVANLEY (1870)

Date opened	22 June 1870
Location	North side of Chester Road (A56)
Company on opening	Cheshire Lines Committee
Date closed to passengers	6 January 1964
Date closed completely	2 March 1964
Company on closing	British Railways (London Midland Region)
Present state	Station building now in use as a private dwelling; platform still intact but obscured by tree growth
County	Cheshire
OS Grid Ref	SJ486747

Helsby & Alvanley station was situated on the Mouldsworth to Helsby Junction line of the Cheshire Lines Committee (CLC), which opened on 1 September 1869; Mouldsworth was on the CLC's Manchester to Chester line. The CLC was jointly owned by the Great Northern Railway (GNR), the Manchester, Sheffield & Lincolnshire Railway (MSLR) and the Midland Railway (MR), and the purpose of this line was to provide the company with access to the Birkenhead Dock system via the Birkenhead Joint Railway (BJR), which had a line that ran from Helsby to Birkenhead. Thus the line was primarily constructed for goods services, but a passenger station was opened at Helsby on 22 June 1870. As the BJR already had a station called Helsby, the CLC's facility was named Helsby & Alvanley.

The line was a single-track branch so the station was provided with one platform on the east side of the track. It had a two-storey brick building that housed all the usual station facilities as well as living accommodation for the station master.

The first passenger service on the line did not prove to be very popular and was withdrawn by the CLC on 1 May 1875, at which time Helsby & Alvanley station closed to passengers.

From October 1936 the station reopened for intermittent use by workmen's services, which operated until 22 May 1944, after which the station closed once again. The timetable for 1943 had one arrival in the morning, which had departed from Hooton at 7.20am, followed by an evening departure that went back to Hooton, leaving Helsby & Alvanley at 6.00pm.

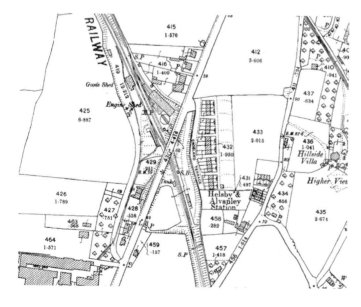

Helsby & Alvanley, 1898

Right: **Helsby & Alvanley:** In the summer of 1949 the station still carried its nameboard despite the fact that this was one of the periods when it was closed to passenger services. In this view looking south the station appears to be remarkably well kept; the occupants of the station house were no doubt eager to keep it in good order. *John Mann collection*

Below: **Helsby & Alvanley:** By January 1980 a steady stream of goods services continued to pass through the station, in particular large quantities of petrochemical products, which were carried until the early 1990s. *John Mann collection*

On nationalisation on 1 January 1948 Helsby & Alvanley station joined British Railways' London Midland Region. A steady stream of goods services continued to pass through the station, and the line gained extra traffic with the opening of a large oil refinery at Stanlow a short distance to the north.

On 9 September 1963, at a time when stations throughout Britain were closing in their hundreds, Helsby & Alvanley reopened as a passenger station, with one train per day leaving at 5.30pm for Rock Ferry. The service lasted only a few months, and on 2 January 1964 the station closed permanently to passenger services. It handled goods services for a few more months before closing completely on 2 March.

Interestingly, the station never appeared as a passenger facility on an Ordnance Survey map in the 20th century.

The line remained busy until 1990, by which time the oil industry had built numerous pipelines from the Stanlow refinery. The commissioning of these pipelines led to a

dramatic drop in the number of freight trains running to and from Stanlow, and the Mouldsworth to Helsby Junction line closed on 14 September 1991. The track remained in situ for a number of years but was eventually lifted. The station passed into private ownership after closure and was still in use as a private residence in 2011.

Helsby & Alvanley: For a number of years after goods services ceased to operate in the early 1990s the line remained in situ, 'mothballed'. In this view, again looking south, in May 1997 the trackbed and platform were very overgrown. *Alan Young*

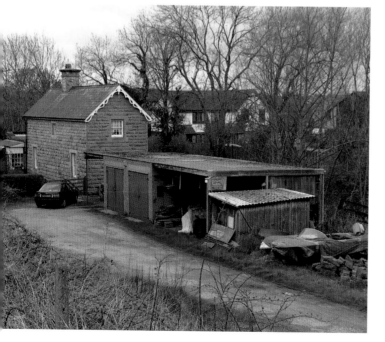

Helsby & Alvanley: The station building survived both the withdrawal of passenger services and the closure of the line. In this view from April 2005 it was being used as a private residence. *Paul Wright*

GARSTON (1874)

Garston station was situated on the Cheshire Lines Committee (CLC) main line between Liverpool Central and Manchester Central. The Cheshire Lines Committee was a joint railway involving the Great Northern Railway (GNR), the Manchester, Sheffield & Lincolnshire Railway (MSLR) and the Midland Railway (MR), with each company holding one-third of the shares. The section of line on which Garston station stood opened from a point just to the west of the station at Cressington Junction to Skelton Junction on 1 August 1873. The CLC had previously had to use the LNWR route through Warrington Arpley to access its terminal facilities at Brunswick in Liverpool from Manchester, and trains using this route had stopped at the nearby station at Garston Dock.

With its own direct route, the CLC was able to open its own Garston station, which it did on 1 April 1874. The station was in a cutting to the west of Woolton Road, and its main entrance consisted of a brick building at street level on the south side of the line.

Date opened	1 April 1874
Location	West side of Woolton Road
Company on opening	Cheshire Lines Committee
Date closed to passengers	10 June 2006
Date closed completely	10 June 2006
Company on closing	Network Rail
Present state	Demolished
County	Lancashire
OS Grid Ref	SJ406848

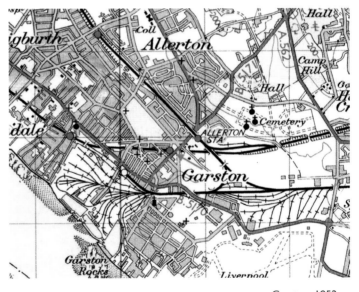

Garston, 1952

The building was single-storey at street level, but two-storey at platform level, and contained booking facilities and storage areas. Steps led down to the westbound platform, which had two single-storey brick buildings that provided waiting facilities, and a two-storey station master's house. A section of canopy supported on iron pillars was provided.

Leading from the street-level booking hall there was a footbridge that gave access to the eastbound platform, which was an island with two faces and provided with an extensive canopy, again supported on iron pillars. Under the canopy there were timber-built waiting rooms. At the east end of the platform was a cast-iron gentlemen's urinal.

At the time of opening Garston station was served by local trains operating to various points along the main line between Liverpool Central and Manchester. The CLC had its own

Garston: The station in the early 20th century. John Mann collection

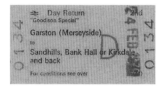

Garston: A Gateacre to Liverpool Central service arrives at Garston in 1969. By this time the station was only served by trains between Liverpool and Gateacre, which were almost always two-car Class 104 DMUs from Allerton shed. *Bevan Price*

Garston: Looking west along the eastbound platform in April 1977, the station had been closed for five years, but in less than a year would reopen as the southern terminus of the Merseyrail Northern Line. Unfortunately the original features seen in this picture were swept away later in the year, and when the station reopened only the former westbound platform, on the left, was used. It was not until the Northern Line was extended to Hunts Cross in 1983 that the eastbound platform came back into use. *Alan Young*

coaches but never had any locomotives, as it had been agreed that the MSLR would provide these. From 1 December 1879 Garston was served by trains between Liverpool Central and Walton-on-the-Hill. From 1884 the station also had services to Southport Lord Street.

Garston developed into a bustling outer suburb of Liverpool and the station was well served to cater for commuter traffic. It was also very close to a market, which generated further passenger traffic.

In 1897 the MSLR changed its name to the Great Central Railway. By this time the CLC had established a fast express service between Liverpool Central and Manchester Central that was well able to compete with its rivals and was known for its excellent punctuality. Most of these express services, however, passed through Garston non-stop.

At the Grouping of 1923 the CLC remained independent, but its owning companies became the London & North Eastern Railway (LNER), with two-thirds of the shares, and the London Midland & Scottish Railway (LMS), which had one-third; the LNER provided the locomotives for the CLC services.

In the summer of 1932 Garston station had 14 weekday services running westbound that had originated from the main line. They had mostly started from Manchester Central and all ran through to Liverpool Central. The

Garston: During its first period of closure between April 1972 and January 1978 the station was allowed to fall into a derelict condition. In this view, looking east in March 1977, the station still retained its original features. *Paul Wright collection*

first departure was at 6.52am and the last at 11.45pm. Going eastbound there were 13 services, most of which ran to Manchester Central. The first departure was at 5.17am and the last at 10.45pm. Garston was also served by a more frequent local service that ran between Gateacre and Liverpool Central, and there were a couple of services to Southport Lord Street.

On 1 January 1948 Garston became part of the nationalised British Railways (London Midland Region), and throughout the 1950s remained a busy suburban station with regular services to Liverpool Central, Gateacre, Warrington Central, Stockport Tiviot Dale and Manchester Central. There were also a couple of peak-hour services to Aintree Central. Many main-line express services also continued to pass through the station. In 1960 diesel multiple units were introduced onto the local services, but the Aintree service ceased on 7 November of that year. The *Reshaping of British Railways* report of 1963 (the 'Beeching Report') recommended the closure of Liverpool Central station and the diversion of all of its main-line services to Liverpool Lime Street. In the April 1966 timetable Garston had 20 trains to Warrington Central, 18 to Gateacre and 43 to Liverpool Central. The first eastbound departure left at 6.34am for Warrington Central, and the first westbound departure was for Liverpool Central at 6.33am. The last train going east was for Warrington Central at 10.04 pm, and the last train for Liverpool Central left at 11.37pm.

In September 1966 all Liverpool Central train services, except those

Garston: The station in its final form is seen looking east from the footbridge in February 2005. The layout of the station in this view dates from 1983 when the line to Hunts Cross reopened as an electrified route for passenger services. *Paul Wright*

serving Gateacre, were diverted to run to Liverpool Lime Street. The diverted trains left the CLC route about a mile east of Garston station, leaving Garston with only the service between Liverpool Central and Gateacre. British Railways wanted to withdraw this service so that it could close Liverpool Central, but opposition from passengers and the local authorities ensured that the service continued. In 1969 the Merseyside Passenger Transport Executive (MPTE) was formed. Building upon reports that had been produced by the local authorities, the MPTE obtained an Act in 1971 that would create what became the Merseyrail network. The line through Garston was to be electrified and linked to an

GARSTON/LIVERPOOL/KIRKBY

Mondays to Saturdays

						SX	SO					
Garston	d		0635	0655	0715	0735	0755	0815	0815	0835	0855	0915 and
Cressington	d		0637	0657	0717	0737	0757	0817	0817	0837	0857	0917 every
Aigburth	d		0639	0659	0719	0739	0759	0819	0819	0839	0859	0919 20
St. Michaels	d		0642	0702	0722	0742	0802	0822	0822	0842	0902	0922 minutes
Liverpool Central	d	0627	0647	0707	0727	0747	0809	0827	0829	0847	0907	0927 until
Moorfields	d	0629	0649	0709	0729	0749	0811	0829	0831	0849	0909	0929
Sandhills	d	0632	0652	0712	0732	0752	0815	0832	0835	0852	0912	0932
Kirkdale	d	0634	0654	0714	0734	0754	0817	0834	0837	0854	0914	0934
Preston Road	d	0638	0658	0718	0738	0758	0820	0838	0840	0858	0918	0938
Fazakerley	d	0641	0701	0721	0741	0801	0823	0841	0843	0901	0921	0941
Kirkby	a	0644	0704	0724	0744	0804	0827	0844	0847	0904	0925	0944

		SO	SX									
Garston	d	1635	1655	1655	1715	1735	1755	1815	1835	1865	1915 and
Cressington	d	1637	1657	1657	1717	1737	1757	1817	1837	1857	1917 every
Aigburth	d	1639	1659	1659	1719	1739	1759	1819	1839	1859	1919 20
St. Michaels	d	1642	1702	1702	1722	1742	1802	1822	1842	1902	1922 minutes
Liverpool Central	d	1647	1707	1710	1727	1747	1809	1827	1847	1907	1927 until
Moorfields	d	1649	1709	1712	1729	1749	1811	1829	1849	1909	1929
Sandhills	d	1652	1712	1715	1732	1752	1815	1832	1852	1912	1932
Kirkdale	d	1654	1714	1717	1734	1754	1817	1834	1854	1914	1934
Preston Road	d	1658	1718	1721	1738	1758	1820	1838	1858	1918	1938
Fazakerley	d	1701	1721	1724	1741	1801	1823	1841	1901	1921	1941
Kirkby	a	1704	1725	1727	1744	1804	1827	1844	1904	1925	1944

					B			
Garston	d	2135	2155	2215		2235	2255	2315
Cressington	d	2137	2157	2217		2237	2257	2317	SX – Saturday excepted
Aigburth	d	2139	2159	2219		2239	2259	2319	SO – Saturdays only
St. Michaels	d	2142	2202	2222		2242	2302	2322	B – to Ormskirk (a) 2354
Liverpool Central	d	2147	2207	2227	2240	2247	2307	2327	a – Arrival time
Moorfields	d	2149	2209	22a29	2242	22a49	2309	2329
Sandhills	d	2152	2212		2246		2312	2332
Kirkdale	d	2154	2214		2248		2314	2334
Preston Road	d	2158	2218		2251		2318
Fazakerley	d	2201	2221		2254		2321
Kirkby	a	2204	2225		2258		2325

Sundays

Garston	d		0904	0934 and		2204	2234
Cressington	d		0906	0936 every		2206	2236
Aigburth	d		0908	0938 30		2208	2238
St. Michaels	d		0910	0940 minutes		2210	2240
Liverpool Central	d	0845	0915	0945 until		2215	2245
Moorfields	d	0847	0917	0947		2217	22a47
Sandhills	d	0850	0920	0950		2220
Kirkdale	d	—	—	—		—
Preston Road	d	—	—	—		—
Fazakerley	d	0856	0926	0956		2226
Kirkby	a	0859	0929	0959		2229

Above: **Garston:** Looking west after closure in July 2006, the benches and lamp columns have already been removed. *Paul Wright*

Above right: **Garston:** Looking east during the final stages of demolition in November 2006, the replacement station can be glimpsed beyond the bridge. *Paul Wright*

underground network in central Liverpool. In order for the construction of the underground lines to take place, Liverpool Central station had to close, and as a result the Gateacre service would have to be withdrawn.

The service was duly discontinued on 17 April 1972 and Garston station was closed. Prior to closure it had been allowed to fall into a poor condition, and after closure it became completely derelict. At some point in the later half of 1977 the street-level building was demolished, together with the footbridge and the extensive station canopies. All structures were removed from the eastbound platform.

Garston station reopened on 3 January 1978 as a terminus station for the Merseyrail network's Northern Line extension. This had seen the line as far as Garston electrified with third rail. Only the former Liverpool-bound platform was in use; the eastbound platform, which had been an island, remained out of use, as did the lines east of Garston. A former platform waiting room was converted into

booking and waiting facilities. In its newly constituted state Garston once again became very busy, having a regular train service to Kirkby via Liverpool Central and the new underground line, which ran at a 20-minute frequency for most of the day.

In 1983 the Northern Line was extended a couple of miles further east to Hunts Cross, where connections with the main line where possible. The island platform was brought back into use, but with only one platform face, and a covered footbridge was provided at the western end of the station. Once again Garston became a through station served by trains running between Hunts Cross and Southport via central Liverpool at a 15-minute frequency.

In the late 1990s Merseytravel, the local authority transport authority, explored the option of creating a new South Liverpool Parkway station, which would serve the former CLC line and the former LNWR main line to London. It was decided to locate the new station just to the east of Garston station – its west-end platform ramps would be less than 10 metres from Garston's east-end ramps.

In the early part of the 21st century work was authorised to create the new station, and on 11 June 2006 South Liverpool Parkway opened. Garston had closed for the second and final time the day before, and was demolished shortly afterwards.

CROSSENS (1878)

Date opened	20 February 1878
Location	East side of Bankfield Lane/Rufford Road
Company on opening	West Lancashire Railway
Date closed to passengers	7 September 1964
Date closed completely	7 September 1964
Company on closing	British Railways (London Midland Region)
Present state	Demolished
County	Lancashire
OS Grid Ref	SD374194

Crossens station was situated on the Southport to Preston line of the West Lancashire Railway (WLR), which opened in stages between 19 February 1878 and 6 September 1882. From the start it struggled financially.

Crossens station opened on 20 February 1878 when the WLR opened the first section of the line from Hesketh Park in Southport to Hesketh Bank. It was located on the north side of a road overbridge that carried Bankfield Road over the line. As the line was double, two platforms were provided. The main station facilities were housed in a single-storey brick building on the west side of the line, on what would become the Preston direction platform. A simple waiting shelter was

Crossens: This view is looking south-east along the Southport-direction platform in the early part of the 20th century. *John Mann collection*

located on the Southport-bound platform. A footbridge at the southern end of the station provided a link between the platforms.

To the north-east of the station on the west side of the line the WLR had its carriage sheds. Land at Southport had been too expensive, so the company developed Crossens as a suitable location.

At the time of opening Crossens was served by trains running between Hesketh Park and Hesketh

Crossens: We are now looking north-east towards Southport in June 1963. Electric services from Southport terminated here, arriving at the Preston-bound platform; after setting down passengers they continued towards Preston for a short distance, then reversed and pulled into the Southport platform. *John Mann collection*

Bank, but on 10 June 1878 the line was extended southwards to Southport Windsor Road. The WLR completed the route to Preston on 6 September 1882, and from that date trains started to run from Crossens to Preston. To coincide with the completion of the route the WLR opened a new terminus at the southern end of the line at Southport Central.

On 1 July 1897 the Lancashire & Yorkshire Railway (LYR) took over the WLR. From 1 May 1901 the LYR closed Southport Central and diverted all WLR line trains into Southport Chapel Street. By this time Crossens had grown into an outlying residential district of Southport, which resulted in the station becoming a busy commuter facility. The LYR decided to extend the electrification that it had planned to carry out between Liverpool Exchange and Southport Chapel Street from Southport to Crossens, and the live rails reached Crossens on 28 February 1904. On 6 March an electric train was run from Crossens to Liverpool, then a full public service began on 5 April. Initially Crossens was served by trains that ran non-stop between Liverpool and Southport, then called at all stations between Southport and Crossens. The electric services arrived at the Preston-direction platform and set down their passengers; they then continued towards the north-east for a short distance to a crossover. The driver would then change ends and draw the train into the Southport platform ready for departure. The station also still had its Preston services.

On 3 June 1912 the LYR introduced a railmotor service that ran between Crossens and Tarleton, which was at the eastern end of a 1½-mile branch that connected the Leeds & Liverpool Canal to the WLR at Hesketh Bank and had opened for goods in 1880. To facilitate the service the signalling was altered so that the railmotor could draw into the north end of the Southport-direction platform, where an electric

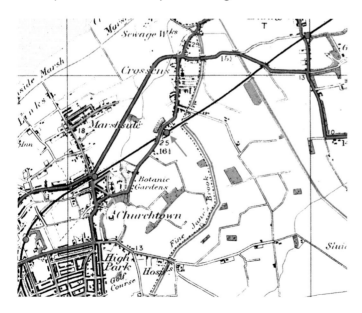

Crossens, 1924

Left: **Crossens:** This is the site of the station looking north-east in August 1984. By this date there was no trace left, and the site had been developed for industrial use. *John Mann collection*

Below: **Crossens:** By February 2006 the site had once again been redeveloped, this time as a residential area. *Bevan Price*

train was already present at the south end. This allowed passengers who arrived from Tarleton to walk just a short distance along the platform to join the electric to Southport. However, the railmotor was not a success and was withdrawn on 1 October 1913.

On 1 January 1922 the LYR was absorbed by the London & North Western Railway, but a year later that company became part of the London Midland & Scottish Railway (LMS). By the summer of 1932 Crossens had 44 weekday electric services to

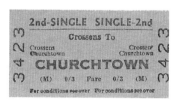

Southport and Preston. During Bank Holidays additional electric services were run.

The *Reshaping of British Railways* report of 1963 recommended the complete closure of the railway from Meols Cop, Southport, through to Preston, including the busy electric section. Despite local protests all services

Southport, which by this time mostly ran as a shuttle service between the two places. These were supplemented by 17 steam-hauled services originating from Preston. There were also 17 trains to Preston, one to Accrington, one to Todmorden and one that was advertised as travelling 'onward to the East Lancashire District'. The first departure from Crossens was for Preston at 5.59am, and the last was for Southport at 11.13pm.

On 1 January 1948 Crossens became part of the nationalised British Railways (London Midland Region), and throughout the 1950s retained its high-frequency electric service together with a good service between

were withdrawn with effect from 7 September 1964 and Crossens station closed completely, as did the line from Hesketh Park to Preston. Track-lifting trains passed through Crossens in the months following closure and a light engine was seen passing through the station as late as 30 January 1965; the line had been completely lifted by April of that year.

The station itself survived in a derelict state for a few more years, but was demolished in the late 1960s. The site was then developed first for industrial use then much later as a residential area.

WIDNES CENTRAL (1879)

Date opened	1 August 1879
Location	North side of Ditton Road, west of Victoria Road
Company on opening	Manchester, Sheffield & Lincolnshire Railway & Midland Railway Joint
Date closed to passengers	5 October 1964
Date closed completely	5 October 1964
Company on closing	British Railways (London Midland Region)
Present state	Demolished; Ashley Way now occupies the site at a much reduced elevation
County	Lancashire
OS Grid Ref	SJ511850

Widnes Central station was situated on the Manchester, Sheffield & Lincolnshire Railway (MSLR) and Midland Railway (MR) Joint Widnes Branch Railway. This ran from a junction on the Cheshire Lines Committee (CLC) Liverpool to Manchester line just east of Hough Green station to another junction on the same line a few miles east of Farnworth station at Widnes East Junction. In effect the line was a loop that provided access to the town of Widnes, which had been bypassed by the CLC.

The MSLR & MR Joint Widnes Branch Railway opened in two stages. The section on which Widnes Central was located opened for goods traffic on 3 April 1877, with the station opening a few years later on 1 August 1879. The station had two platforms and was situated on an embankment above street level to the west of Victoria Road. An approach road connected Ditton Road to the main station facilities, which were situated on the Liverpool (westbound) platform. The buildings were single-storey brick structures and included a substantial canopy over the platform. A subway connected to the Warrington (eastbound) platform, which was also provided with a brick building and a canopy. A path also connected the

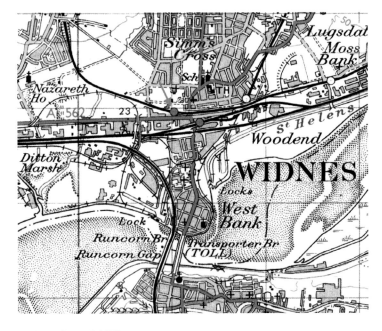

Widnes Central, 1952

Above: **Widnes Central:** Looking west along the Liverpool-bound platform in 1956, the station appears to be clean and tidy, and a porter can be seen carrying boxes. During this period many small packages were sent to and dispatched from stations like Widnes Central. *John Mann collection*

Below: **Widnes Central:** This early 1960s view looking west from an elevated position shows that the station was situated on an embankment high above the nearby factories and other businesses. It was provided with two platforms linked by a subway, and its main facilities were located on the westbound platform, which was connected to Ditton Road by its own approach road, as seen here. *Gordon Howarth*

eastbound platform to street level.

At the time of opening Widnes Central station was served by trains operated by both of the owning companies and by CLC services. The CLC was owned by three companies: the MSLR and the MR, together with the Great Northern Railway. It never owned any locomotives, so its services were hauled by MSLR motive power. Passengers could travel from Widnes Central to Liverpool, Manchester, Warrington and Southport and to points further afield.

On 1 September 1890 another station opened on the Widnes branch; located just over a mile to the east of Widnes Central, it was called Tanhouse Lane.

On 1 July 1897 the MSLR changed its name to the Great Central Railway (GCR) and Widnes Central became part of the GCR & MR Widnes Branch. At the Grouping of 1923 the GCR became part of the London & North Eastern Railway (LNER) and the MR part of the London Midland & Scottish Railway (LMS). The CLC remained as a separate company owned jointly by the LMS, with a one-third share, and the LNER, with two-thirds. CLC services through Widnes Central were hauled by LNER locomotives. The LMS Summer timetable for 1932 shows that they operated services from Widnes Central to Southport Lord Street, Manchester Central and Stockport Tiviot Dale. However, most trains were CLC services running between Liverpool Central and Manchester Central.

On 1 January 1948 Widnes Central passed into British Railways (London Midland Region) hands. By the summer of 1957 most services ran between Liverpool Central and Manchester Central or Warrington Central. There were nine eastbound services on Monday to Friday; the first, at 7.00am, only went to Tanhouse Lane, while the last, at 7.18pm, went to Warrington Central. There were no eastbound services between 12.07pm and 5.22pm.

In the westbound direction there were 11 trains on Monday to Friday; the first was at 6.59am and the last at 9.01pm, both going to Liverpool Central. Unlike

Widnes Central: This view was taken from the westbound platform looking at the facilities opposite in 1964 shortly before the station's closure. It is quite clear that the station had been allowed to fall into a state of disrepair by this time. Towards the right of the picture the entrance to the subway can be seen, indicated by a directional sign. *Gordon Howarth*

Widnes Central: The main entrance is seen looking east towards the station approach road in October 1964. *David Nicholas*

the eastbound service, there was no big gap in services during the afternoon. On Saturdays there were 12 westbound services. No service operated in either direction on Sundays.

By the time the winter timetable for 1964 appeared the station had only five eastbound and six westbound services between Monday and Friday. The first eastbound service was at 6.57am and went only as far as Tanhouse Lane; the last was at 6.18pm and went to Warrington Central. Westbound, the first service was for Liverpool Central at 6.51am, and the last, also for Liverpool Central, left at 6.32pm. Remarkably, between the hours of 8.33am and 5.17pm Widnes Central had no trains at all on weekdays.

On Saturdays the westbound service was a little better, with seven services to Liverpool Central, but the eastbound was worse, with only four services. There was not such a long gap in the daytime on Saturdays as there was a Liverpool Central service at 1.43pm. However, one train between 8.33am and 5.17pm was hardly likely to persuade passengers to make use of the station. This was probably the intention, as the line had been recommended for closure in the *Reshaping of British Railways* report of 1963. No service at all operated on Sundays.

Widnes Central: Saturday 3 October 1964 was the last day that passenger services operated, as Sunday services had long since ceased. The train is a midday Saturday service for Liverpool Central, which proved very popular with shoppers who could have an afternoon in Liverpool. Fairburn 4MT 2-6-4T No 42064 was based at Trafford Park in Manchester, and is attached to a rake of pre-war suburban coaches that were typical of the local trains that ran on routes out of Liverpool Central before DMUs were introduced. *Neville Conroy*

The last full day of train services was Saturday 3 October 1964, and the last service to leave was the 4.56pm to Manchester Central, a steam-hauled train of five coaches. Four minutes earlier the last westbound service had left for Liverpool Central, this train being a two-coach DMU. Widnes Central station officially closed on 5 October.

Shortly after closure the line was also closed, goods services being diverted along other routes. The station was demolished apart from its platforms, and the track was lifted. For many years after closure the embankment and viaduct on which the station stood survived in a derelict condition, but all was swept away in 1984 to make way for a new road. Today nothing remains of the station.

Above: **Widnes Central:** This view is looking east at the site of the station shortly after its platforms had been demolished in the early 1980s. The route of the line towards Warrington can be seen heading off into the distance. By 1984 all trace of the line had been swept away as part of the construction of Ashley Way. *John Mann collection*

Below: **Widnes Central:** The site of the station is seen in February 2006 looking east. In 1983 the embankment on which it had stood was demolished and Ashley Way, which opened in 1984, was constructed through the station site. *Paul Wright*

GATEACRE (1879)

Date opened	1 December 1879
Location	Belle Vale Road
Company on opening	Cheshire Lines Committee
Date closed to passengers	15 April 1972
Date closed completely	15 April 1972
Company on closing	British Rail (London Midland Region)
Present state	Demolished; trackbed now forms part of Liverpool Loop Line Cycle Path
County	Lancashire
OS Grid Ref	SJ429879

Gateacre station was located on the Cheshire Lines Committee's North Liverpool Extension Line. The CLC was a joint railway consisting of three partners, the Manchester, Sheffield & Lincolnshire Railway (MSLR), the Midland Railway (MR) and the Great Northern Railway (GNR). The North Liverpool Extension Line was authorised on 30 July 1874 and work commenced on its construction in August the following year. The purpose of the line was to provide a connection from the CLC's main Liverpool to Manchester line to the deep-water berths of the rapidly expanding north Liverpool docks. The CLC chose a route for the line that skirted through agricultural land to the east of Liverpool, running from a junction with the CLC main line at Halewood and passing through small villages at Gateacre, Knotty Ash, West Derby and Walton before terminating at Huskisson.

Gateacre station was close to and on the eastern side of its village namesake, and opened to both goods and passenger services on 1 December 1879. The line was on an embankment, and the station was located on the north side of Belle Vale Road, which passed under the line. The station's layout was unusual in that the main building was set back away from the line on the western side; the reason for this was that although the CLC North

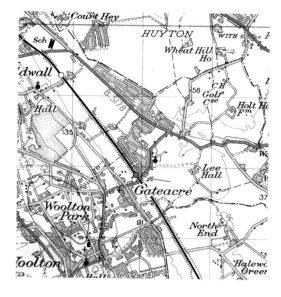

Gateacre, 1952

Liverpool Extension Line had been built as a double-track railway it was anticipated that it would need to be quadrupled at some point in the future. Therefore to avoid unnecessary expense the CLC purchased enough land to undertake the quadrupling, and built its stations, overbridges and tunnels in a way that would accommodate the future plans. As things worked out the line was never quadrupled. The

main station building was of brick and consisted of two storeys containing the main booking office and living accommodation for the station master.

The station was reached by a sloping path from Belle Vale Road and, being set away from the line, a covered timber walkway provided a link to the northbound platform. The latter was constructed from a timber edge backfilled with earth and topped off with cinders and in part with tiles. A large wooden canopy was provided towards the southern end of the platform.

The southbound platform was connected to the main station building by a subway. It also had a large wooden canopy that mirrored that on the northbound platform, and timber-built waiting facilities were located at the rear of the canopy area.

Just to the south of the station platforms was the Belle Vale bridge, and south of that on the east side of the line was the timber-built Gateacre signal box. Opposite the box

Gateacre: A train for Aintree Central arrives on 5 November 1960, the last day that services between Aintree Central and Manchester Central would operate. The following day Gateacre became a terminus station served only by trains to Liverpool Central. In this picture the station is seen in its 'modernised' form, having lost its extensive canopies in the 1950s. Jim Peden

Gateacre: This view looking north from Belle Vale Road towards the station in the early part of the 20th century shows the main station building and how it was situated away from the line to allow for possible quadrupling, which was never carried out. A covered walkway linked the building to the northbound platform, and a subway provided a link to the southbound platform. John Mann collection

was Gateacre's goods facilities, which consisted of sidings reached by a driveway from the southern side of Belle Vale Road.

At the time of opening Gateacre station was served by 12 trains each day, which ran between Liverpool Central and Walton-on-the-Hill; on 13 July 1880 the service was extended to Huskisson, when construction of the final section of the line was completed. The CLC provided the services using its own coaches, but it had no locomotives, as the partner companies had agreed that the MSLR would provide them.

On 1 September 1884 a further northward extension of the route opened to Southport Lord Street, and

Gateacre: A Liverpool Central service waits to depart in 1971. The station was showing signs of neglect at this time, and despite the best efforts of local people to save the service it was withdrawn on 15 April 1972 and Gateacre station closed. *Alan Young collection*

Gateacre: Looking east from the booking office window towards the subway in the early 1960s, chalk Boards provide passengers with ticket price information. *David Nicholas*

from that date services also began to run from Liverpool Central and Manchester Central to Southport Lord Street. On 1 May 1885 the Huskisson service was cut back to Walton-on-the-Hill. From 1887 the station was being

Gateacre: This is the view looking north along the former northbound platform on 3 April 1977. The line had been out of use since August 1975, and passenger services had ceased to operate in April 1972. The last trains to pass through the station were trip freight workings operating between Edge Hill and Huskisson. The CLC North Liverpool Extension Line had been reduced in stages to a single-track, one-train-in-operation branch by 1973, and was lifted in the early months of 1979. *Alan Young*

referred to as Gateacre for Woolton. (Woolton was a larger village a short distance to the south-west of Gateacre). In 1897 the MSLR was renamed as the Great Central Railway (GCR).

During the Great War the North Liverpool Extension Line was very busy with goods services and troop trains, as many military camps were located adjacent to the line. However, on 1 January 1917 the Southport service was cut back to run only as far as Aintree, and on 1 January 1918 the Liverpool Central and Walton-on-the-Hill service was withdrawn completely, leaving only services to Aintree, Liverpool Central and Manchester Central. On

1 April 1919 passenger services to Southport Lord Street were reinstated, and a local stopping service between Gateacre for Woolton and Liverpool Central had become established by this time, running more frequently than the other services.

At the time of the Grouping in 1923 the CLC remained independent, but its controlling

Gateacre: As seen in this view looking south at the station site in February 2005, the route of the line through Gateacre was developed as the Liverpool Loop Line Cycleway in the early 1990s. During the construction of the cycleway the platform edges were demolished and mounds created on either side of the path to provide privacy for residents whose properties back onto the site of the station. *Paul Wright*

Gateacre: Looking east towards the Belle Vale bridge, the station was located to the left, accessed by a path that started by the railings. *Paul Wright*

shareholders became the London & North Eastern Railway (LNER), with two-thirds of the shares, and the London Midland & Scottish Railway (LMS), with one-third. The CLC continued to own its own coaches but locomotives for local services were now provided by the LNER.

In the summer of 1932 Gateacre for Woolton station had nine trains to Southport Lord Street and seven to Manchester Central on weekdays. In addition, it had a regular service to Liverpool Central, which commenced at Gateacre. There were also a couple of services that originated at Southport and went through to Liverpool Central. The first departure for Southport Lord Street was at 7.18am and the first for Manchester at 8.19am. The last service for Southport was at 7.49pm and the last for Manchester left at 9.02pm.

During the Second World War the line through Gateacre for Woolton was once again extremely busy with war traffic. Then on 1 January 1948 the railways were nationalised and Gateacre for Woolton became part of British Railways (London Midland Region). On 7 January 1952 BR closed the line from

Aintree to Southport to passenger services, so from that date the only northbound services from Gateacre for Woolton were to Aintree, which had been renamed as Aintree Central in 1950. Most of these services originated from Manchester Central, but there were a couple of peak-hour trains that originated from Liverpool Central. Going southbound the most frequent service was the regular stopping train to Liverpool Central. A more sparse service operated to Manchester Central, having originated from Aintree Central.

In the 1950s Gateacre for Woolton station lost its large wooden canopies, and its platforms were rebuilt in concrete. A short simple shelter was provided on the northbound platform and a simple waiting room on the southbound one. By 1956 the station was being referred to simply as Gateacre.

By the end of the 1950s there were very few passenger trains operating north to Aintree Central from Gateacre, and the service was withdrawn on 7 November 1960, leaving only the Gateacre to Liverpool Central service, which by that date had been handed over to modern diesel multiple units. Passenger services could still be seen running northwards through Gateacre once a year on Grand National Race Day until 1966.

The *Reshaping of British Railways* report of 1963, the 'Beeching Report', recommended the withdrawal of passenger services from Gateacre. However, there was strong local opposition and the entire North Liverpool Extension Line had been the subject of local authority reports, recommending that it be developed and reopened in its entirety to passenger services. Meanwhile, the goods facilities at Gateacre closed on 4 December 1965.

With effect from 18 April 1966 Gateacre had 18 weekday services to Liverpool Central, with a few extra trains on Saturdays but none on Sundays, and the service was allocated to two-car DMUs, based at Allerton. By the end of 1966 the Gateacre service was the only one using the large terminus at Liverpool Central, which made it very costly to operate. In 1968

there was a bus strike in Liverpool, and the Gateacre trains carried thousands of extra passengers, which further demonstrated their potential.

On 1 April 1969 the Merseyside Passenger Transport Executive was created and, building upon the work undertaken by the local authorities, was successful in gaining powers that would completely change the railway network in Liverpool through the creation of links that would create what became the Merseyrail network. The line through Gateacre was included in the proposals with the intention that it be electrified.

In order to facilitate the construction of underground lines in the centre of Liverpool, it was necessary to close Liverpool Central station, and as a result the Gateacre service was withdrawn on 15 April 1972, supposedly as a temporary measure to allow loop and link underground tunnels, which were to be a key feature of the Merseyrail network, to be completed. The station buildings were demolished soon after closure, but the platforms remained extant.

The original intention that Gateacre would reopen complete with electrification as part of the Merseyrail network was not to be. Although the line did reopen from Liverpool Central to Garston in 1978, and onwards to Hunts Cross in 1983, an economic slowdown had already ended any ideas of reopening the line through Gateacre.

Steadily goods traffic on the line declined, and in 1973 it was singled from Hunts Cross to West Derby, having been singled from West Derby to Huskisson a few years earlier. The last goods trains ran in August 1975, and the line was lifted by a demolition train over a number of Sundays in early 1979.

In the late 1980s and early 1990s the route of the North Liverpool Extension Line was developed as the Liverpool Loop Line Path; this formed part of the National Cycleway Network Route 62, also known as the Trans Pennine Trail. During the construction of the path the platforms were demolished.

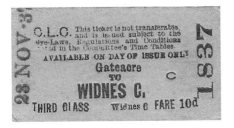

WALTON-ON-THE-HILL (1879)

Date opened	1 December 1879
Location	Junction of Rice Lane and Queens Drive
Company on opening	Cheshire Lines Committee
Date closed to passengers	1 January 1918
Date closed completely	9 September 1968
Company on closure to passengers	Cheshire Lines Committee
Present state	Demolished
County	Lancashire
OS Grid Ref	SJ360950

Walton-on-the-Hill station was situated at the northern end of the North Liverpool Extension Line of the Cheshire Lines Committee (CLC). The CLC was a joint railway consisting of three partners, the Manchester, Sheffield & Lincolnshire Railway (MSLR), the Midland Railway (MR) and the Great Northern Railway (GNR). The North Liverpool Extension Line was authorised on 30 July 1874, and work commenced on its construction in August 1875. Its purpose was to connect the CLC's Liverpool to Manchester line with the deep-water berths of the rapidly expanding north Liverpool docks, and its a route skirted through agricultural land to the east of Liverpool, from a junction with the CLC main line at Halewood through Gateacre to Walton. From Walton it turned south-west and ran down to the docks to terminate at Huskisson Dock. The only major civil engineering on the line was required at Walton, where three tunnels had to be dug to carry the line through the sandstone ridge that surrounds the city of Liverpool.

Walton-on-the-Hill station opened to passenger services on 1 December 1879. At this time the line through to Huskisson was not complete, so the station acted as a terminus. It was situated in a cutting at the north-eastern end of the Walton tunnels, and since the line was double track it was provided with two platforms. Public access was via a single-storey building that sat on top of the tunnel mouth on Rice Lane and ramps that led to the platforms Facilities at platform level were basic, consisting of a brick-built shelter on the Liverpool

Walton on the Hill, 1923

Above: **Walton-on-the-Hill:**
The station is seen looking
north-east in the early 1930s.
Beyond the platforms to the
right can be seen the Walton-on-
the-Hill locomotive sheds. *John
Mann collection*

Right: **Walton-on-the-Hill:**
Looking north-east again in 1950,
a goods train for Huskisson
approaches the station. *John
Mann collection*

platform, and a smaller
shelter on the Huskisson
platform. At the north-
eastern end of the Liverpool-
bound platform there was
a signal box that controlled
traffic movements through the station.

At the time of opening 12 trains each day
ran to Liverpool Central. On 13 July 1880
the service was extended to run through to
Huskisson, as construction of the final section
of the line had been completed. The same day
marked the opening of a line that had actually
been completed by December 1879, from what
became Fazakerley South Junction to Aintree.

On 13 May 1881 the CLC opened an
engine shed adjacent to the Huskisson
platform, on the east side of the line at the
north-east end of the station. A few years
later, in 1884, a curve was opened from a
point a little to the north-east of Walton-
on-the-Hill station, at what became known
as Fazakerley West Junction, which provided
a direct connection to the Aintree line at
Fazakerley North Junction, thus creating a
triangle of lines to the north-east of the station
allowing trains from Walton-on-the-Hill and
Huskisson to travel both northwards to Aintree
and southwards to Halewood – although the
passenger service from Walton-on-the-Hill
only travelled southward. Within the triangle of
lines sidings were laid out and the area became
known locally as the Walton Triangle. From 1
September 1884 the Aintree line was extended

Above: **Walton-on-the-Hill:**
Looking south-west towards Huskisson in July 1961, the station platforms are in remarkably good condition considering that they have not seen regular passenger services for 43 years. The building on the left is part of the Walton-on-the-Hill motive power depot.
John D. Rodgers

Right: **Walton-on-the-Hill:**
Another view from July 1961, looking from above the tunnel mouth. *John D. Rodgers*

to Southport, and after that date most passenger services on the CLC North Liverpool Extension Line bypassed Walton-on-the-Hill and ran along the new line.

Huskisson station was only about 3 miles from the centre of Liverpool, but a journey by rail to Liverpool Central involved travelling a circuitous route of about 16 miles. A short distance from Huskisson was Sandhills station on the Lancashire & Yorkshire Railway's main line between Liverpool Exchange and Bolton, and a journey from Sandhills to Liverpool took only a few minutes. Because of this, Huskisson was, as a passenger station, a financial disaster,

and closed on 1 May 1885. From this date Walton-on-the-Hill became a terminus for passenger services once again, and by 1910 only four trains ran to and from Liverpool Central, calling at all stations along the North Liverpool Extension Line.

Walton-on-the-Hill passenger station closed on 1 January 1918, a very early casualty of road competition. The station was maintained in good order after this date, as it was conveniently situated close to Walton-on-the-

Walton-on-the-Hill: Three years later in 1964, despite having now been closed for 46 years, the station's platforms are still remarkably intact. They would survive until the early 1980s. *Dave Nicholas*

Hill engine shed and could be used by engine crews as a means of joining or leaving engines that were en route to or from the docks. Although the passenger service had failed to be profitable, the line itself proved to be very lucrative, with a steady stream of goods services passing through the station site.

At the Grouping of British railways into four companies in 1923, the CLC remained independent but its owners became the London & North Eastern Railway (LNER), with two-thirds, and the London Midland & Scottish (LMS) with one-third.

Walton-on-the-Hill station was used occasionally for excursion trains during the 1920s and the 1930s, and during the war the line became even busier as the docks at Liverpool became the gateway for the Atlantic trade with the United States. Millions of tons of war materials passed through the site of Walton-on-the-Hill station during the conflict.

With nationalisation on 1 January 1948 Walton-on-the-Hill became part of the London Midland Region of British Railways. In the 1960s goods traffic began to decline, and on 15 December 1963 Walton-on-the-Hill engine shed closed, its remaining allocation of engines being transferred to Aintree. On 13 June 1964 Walton-on-the-Hill station was visited by a Liverpool University Public Transport Society enthusiasts' special, which was probably

the last time a passenger train called at the station. In 1965 the line was singled from a point just to the north-east of the station through to Huskisson. On 9 September 1968 the station and the yards at the Walton Triangle formally closed for goods services.

On 5 January 1970 the line to Aintree was closed and lifted, and the remaining line towards Halewood was singled between Walton-on-the-Hill and West Derby. The last scheduled goods trains passed through the site of Walton-on-the-Hill station in August 1975, yet despite the absence of trains the station remained virtually intact during numerous visits by the author between 1975 and 1980, as did Walton-on-the-Hill shed. The remaining single track passing through the station was formally taken out of use on 11th February 1979 and lifted a few weeks

Walton-on-the-Hill: This is the station site in August 1995. The station platforms stretched right up to the tunnel mouth; two ramps ran up to the top of the tunnel and a footpath connected the platforms. *Paul Wright*

Left: **Walton-on-the-Hill:** A similar view looking south-west towards the tunnel in February 2010. *Paul Wright*

Below: **Walton-on-the-Hill:** Also in February 2010, the photographer is now standing on the site of the original station building, which sat across the tracks on top of Walton-on-the-Hill No 1 Tunnel. The footpath that can be seen at the bottom of the picture ran across the top of the tunnel and gave access to the platforms via ramps. To the centre right the building that can be made out behind the trees stands on the site of Walton-on-the-Hill locomotive shed. *Paul Wright*

later. After 1981 part of the station site, the site of the shed and the Walton Triangle were developed as a housing estate. The station was demolished at this time, the trackbed partly filled in, and the tunnel mouth bricked up and gates fitted. Today the part of the station site that was not developed and the tunnel mouth are secured from public access by palisade fencing.

WITHINGTON & WEST DIDSBURY (1880)

Date opened	1 January 1880
Location	North-east side of Lapwing Lane
Company on opening	Midland Railway
Date closed to passengers	3 July 1961
Date closed completely	3 July 1961
Company on closing	British Railways (London Midland Region)
Present state	Demolished, and site heavily overgrown
County	Lancashire
OS Grid Ref	SJ842923

Withington & West Didsbury station opened as Withington on 1 January 1880 as part of the Manchester South District Railway, which connected Manchester Central with Stockport Tiviot Dale.

A number of schemes had been proposed to create a line from Manchester through Didsbury and down towards Stockport from as early as 1864. In 1873 the Manchester South District Railway (MSDR) obtained an Act to create a line from Manchester via Didsbury to Alderley. A year later, on 30 June 1874, the MDSR obtained a variation Act proposing that the line would make a connection with the Cheshire Lines Committee (CLC) route between Woodley and Skelton Junction at Heaton Mersey. However, despite obtaining the Act the MDSR was unable to start work on the construction of the line due to financial difficulties. At this point the CLC became interested in purchasing the MDSR, as it saw value in the projected route to Manchester. Unfortunately one of the partners, the Great Northern Railway (GNR), did not agree, so the CLC was unable to proceed with its idea.

Withington & West Didsbury: The station is seen looking south along the southbound platform in the first decade of the 20th century. The generous protection provided by the spacious canopies is clearly shown. The station was well used as a means of commuting into central Manchester. *John Mann collection*

The other two CLC partners, the Manchester, Sheffield & Lincolnshire Railway (MSLR) and the Midland Railway (MR) decided to press ahead and purchase the MSDR. The MR in particular wanted a route of its own into Manchester so that it was not beholden to other companies;

since 1867 its train services from the south had had to use Manchester London Road station, which was jointly owned by the London & North Western Railway (LNWR) and the MSLR. A bill was granted by Parliament on 11 August 1876 authorising the MR and MSLR to take over the MSDR and build the line from Heaton Mersey to Manchester. Within a month of the Act being signed the MSLR got cold feet and decided that it did not want to proceed. The MR was still desperate to create a route of its own into Manchester, and to make matters worse it had been given notice to quit London Road station. So the MR went back to Parliament and on 12 July 1877 was given authority to take over the MSDR and build the line.

Work began in 1878. Withington was the second intermediate station on the line from Manchester Central and was located about a mile from Withington itself on the western edge

Withington & West Didsbury, 1953

of Didsbury, in a shallow cutting on the north-east side of Lapwing Lane. It was provided with two platforms and the main station building was located on the northbound platform; the latter was a brick building in a Gothic style and was similar to the design used at Didsbury station. It was mostly single-storey but included a two-storey station master's house to the right of the main station entrance. Booking facilities, a parcels office, ladies' and gentlemen's waiting rooms and toilets were all accommodated in the building. An iron footbridge complete with roof gave access to the southbound platform. Both platforms were provided with canopies giving shelter from the weather. A signal box was located to the north of the station a few metres from the ramp of the southbound platform.

Withington & West Didsbury: A southbound South District service arrives in 1909. It will have started its journey at Manchester Central and will be travelling to either Stockport Tiviot Dale or Cheadle Heath. *John Alsop collection*

When the station opened on 1 January 1880 it was served by trains that called at all stations between Manchester Central and Manchester London Road via Stockport Tiviot Dale. Fourteen trains ran in each direction, and Withington station became very busy. The local service was known as the South District Service.

The main reason why the MR had wanted to build the South District Line was to give it access to Manchester without the need to use lines not in its control. From August

1880, therefore, the MR started to run express trains between Manchester Central and London St Pancras via the South District line. These trains passed through Withington but did not stop, as the station was regarded as very much a local facility.

On 1 July 1884 the MR renamed the station as Withington & Albert Park, a name change designed to attract business from the new housing development of Albert Park. The line became busier and busier and the South District Service became more frequent, eventually running every 10 minutes in each direction.

In 1900 Manchester Corporation completed an electric tramway to Withington, which passed close to the station. The introduction of the trams had a big effect on passenger business, which had declined by a third by 1910.

On 1 October 1901 the MR opened part of a new line between Heaton Mersey and New Mills to provide a faster route to the south for express services, and from that date half of the South District services began to run to a new station at Cheadle Heath, which was provided as an interchange station so that passengers could transfer between long-distance and local trains. Express services were using the new route by July 1902.

Withington & West Didsbury: Another view from the same period, showing a crowded platform and an approaching northbound train. *John Alsop collection*

Withington & Albert Park continued to be served by a steady stream of South District passenger trains, and the service settled into a regular pattern with most trains running between Manchester Central and Stockport Tiviot Dale or Cheadle Heath. On 1 April 1915 the MR renamed Withington & Albert Park as Withington & West Didsbury. The Great War led to a reduction in services, but by 1922 things had started to return to normal.

In 1923 Withington & West Didsbury station became part of the London Midland & Scottish Railway (LMS). Because of the competition from the trams and later from buses the station was one of the least busy on the line.

In 1948 the station became part of the nationalised British Railways (London Midland Region), and by the 1950s the South District services had gone into serious decline.

Withington & West Didsbury: Looking north in early British Railways days, the station was still served by a steady stream of local services running between Manchester, Stockport and Cheadle Heath. Main-line express services running between Manchester Central and London St Pancras also passed through the station. *John Mann collection*

Withington & West Didsbury:
In April 2010 the platforms
emerged from beneath heavy
vegetation as the route of the
former Midland Railway was
cleared in preparation for the
creation of a new line of the
Manchester Metrolink tram
system. In this view looking east, a
section of the former southbound
platform can be seen, and at the
rear of the platform can be seen
the remains of a waiting room.
Paul Wright

Withington & West Didsbury:
We are now looking south-east
from the site of the main station
building in April 2010 during
construction works associated
with the creation of the
Manchester Metrolink tram route.
Paul Wright

Trains that had consisted of seven coaches were
reduced to four, and by 1956 the service was
reduced to 16 trains a day in each direction,
only two more than had run at the time of
the station's opening in 1880. There was no
reduction in express services, though. From
1958 work began on the electrification of the
former LNWR route from Manchester to
London, and as a result even more traffic was
routed along the former MR line.

Early in 1961 diesel multiple units (DMUs)
were introduced on the South District locals,
but they were unable to save Withington &
West Didsbury station. It was only being used
by a handful of passengers each day so BR
decided to close it to passenger services on 3
July 1961.

The South District local services continued
to operate until 2 January 1967. By this time the
electrification of the LNWR route to London

was complete and traffic was concentrated
on that line. The last express service along the
South District line ran on 1 January 1968, and
from that date only two passenger trains per
week were scheduled to run through the site
of Withington & West Didsbury; they finished
on Sunday 4 May 1969 when the very last train
services operated out of Manchester Central.
The odd freight train continued to pass through
the station site during the summer of 1969,
but on 17 August the line was disconnected
at Chorlton Junction, and lifted in 1970.
Withington & West Didsbury station was
demolished at the end of the 1960s and today a
block of flats called Lapwing Court occupies the
site. The route of the line through the station
site has been converted into a line of the
Manchester Metrolink tramway.

DEAN LANE (1880)

Date opened	17 May 1880
Location	East side of Dean Lane
Company on opening	Lancashire & Yorkshire Railway
Date closed to passengers	3 October 2009
Date closed completely	3 October 2009
Company on closing	Network Rail
Present state	Platforms and basic shelters survive; all original buildings have gone
County	Lancashire
OS Grid Ref	879008

Dean Lane station was opened by the Lancashire & Yorkshire Railway (LYR) on 17 May 1880 as part of the Thorpes Bridge Junction to Oldham Werneth line. The purpose of the line was to provide a direct route from Manchester to Oldham that avoided a steep incline on the existing LYR line to Oldham via Middleton.

The Thorpes Bridge to Oldham Werneth line had originally been proposed in 1848. It was resurveyed ten years later in 1858, but it was not until 13 January 1875 that the LYR authorised the funding for its construction. On 30 June a contract was let to a Mr Evans and work commenced on 2 August 1876. Mr Evans employed 450 men to construct the line, which was completed by 1880; it created a through route to Rochdale via Oldham, which became known as the Oldham Loop.

Dean Lane station was 2¾ miles from Manchester Victoria on the east side of its namesake. As the line was a double-track railway, the station was provided with two platforms. It had a single-storey brick booking office at street level on the south side of the line, and covered steps led down to the Manchester platform, which was provided with a canopy and a single-storey building providing waiting facilities and a ladies' toilet. A covered footbridge also crossed the line from the street-level booking office to the Oldham-bound platform, where brick waiting facilities and a short canopy were provided.

At the time of its opening Dean Lane was served by 15 trains towards Oldham and 15 to Manchester Victoria. On 1 January 1922 Dean Lane station became part of the London & North Western Railway (LNWR) when that company took over the LYR. However, on 1 January 1923 the LNWR was in turn absorbed into the London Midland & Scottish

Dean Lane, 1953

Dean Lane: An Oldham Loop stopping service bound for Rochdale arrives at Dean Lane in April 1957. Although by this date the station had lost its original canopies all of the other facilities were still present. *H. C. Casserley*

Railway (LMS). By 1938 Dean Lane station was still being served by 15 local trains. There was also a Friday-evening-only train that ran to Glasgow and Edinburgh via Rochdale, a Sunday-only train that originated at Royton and ran on to Blackpool Central via Manchester Victoria, and a Sunday-only train that started from Milnrow and ran to Southport via Manchester Victoria.

On 1 January 1948 Dean Lane became part of the nationalised British Railways (London Midland Region). During the last year of fully steam-operated services in 1958 there were 18 trains in each direction between Manchester and Rochdale. In June of that year BR introduced diesel multiple units (DMUs) on the Oldham Loop in the form of Cravens-built units (later known as Class 104) that had twin power cars so were easily able to cope with the steep gradients. The service pattern at Dean Lane was a train every 20 minutes to Manchester and northbound trains also every 20 minutes. The northbound destinations alternated with a service to Rochdale every 40

Dean Lane: Looking west in October 1959, on the far side of the bridge can be glimpsed Newton Heath motive power depot; two railway workers are walking towards the depot from the station. It was common practice for railway staff to use Dean Lane as a means of access to the depot, but in the station's latter years, when health and safety regulations were tighter, the practice was forbidden. *H. C. Casserley*

Above: **Dean Lane:** The British Rail corporate image sign at the entrance to the station in April 1984. *John Mann collection*

Left: **Dean Lane:** By April 1984 the station had been reduced to a basic unstaffed halt. 'Bus shelter'-style waiting areas were the only provision for inclement weather. *John Mann collection*

minutes and a service to Royton, also every 40 minutes. In total there were 29 trains running between Manchester and Rochdale, and 25 between Manchester and Royton. This was the highest frequency of service that Dean Lane ever enjoyed.

September 1964 saw a decline in services, and following the 'Beeching Report' of 1963 the service between Manchester and Rochdale became irregular, but with trains calling at Dean Lane about every 45 minutes in each direction. Trains between Royton and Manchester Victoria were reduced to seven on a weekday in each direction, eight in each direction on a Saturday and none on Sundays.

From April 1966 further changes took place, including the closure of the Royton branch. The service pattern was altered so that most trains serving Dean Lane ran between Manchester Victoria and Oldham Mumps, with fewer

continuing onward to Rochdale. By 1968 the Dean Lane service had settled into a 30-minute frequency in each direction. However, going north only every other train continued beyond Oldham Mumps to Rochdale, giving only an hourly frequency to that town.

In a note published in the May 1973 timetable, passengers using Dean Lane station were informed that the Secretary of State had given consent to the withdrawal of passenger services between Oldham Mumps and Rochdale. However, by this date the South

Dean Lane: The Manchester direction platform is seen from a passing eastbound train in July 1985. *Alan Young*

East Lancashire North East Cheshire (SELNEC) Passenger Transport Executive (Greater Manchester Passenger Transport Executive – GMPTE – from April 1974) had stepped in and agreed to fund the continuation of the service.

The buildings at Dean Lane were demolished in the 1970s and simple 'bus shelters' were provided. From the introduction of the May 1979 timetable the trains that ran only as far as Oldham Mumps were extended to run further north to Shaw & Crompton. The service pattern at Dean Lane remained as a train every 30 minutes in each direction, and it remained as such until the May 1989 timetable, when a half-hourly service to Rochdale was introduced with extra services at peak hours to Shaw & Crompton.

In May 1995 the last alteration was made to the train services that called at Dean Lane. From that date the station was served by a half-hourly train in each direction that connected Manchester Victoria with Shaw & Crompton. Rochdale trains continued to run, at a half-hourly frequency in each direction, but they passed through Dean Lane without stopping.

During the mid-1990s the GMPTE had been looking at extending its 1992-opened Metrolink tram system. One idea that had been considered as early as 1984 was using the Oldham Loop as a means of extending tram services to Oldham and Rochdale. By the

Dean Lane: A Freightliner train heads east through the station on its way to the Dean Lane waste transfer site in September 2009. Hauled by a Class 66 locomotive, it is taking empty waste containers back to the transfer site for loading with domestic refuse. Once loaded the train will head back through Dean Lane station heading west. *Bevan Price*

beginning of the 21st century plans had been drawn up and a few years later funding was in place to carry out the required works. To enable the works to go ahead the Oldham Loop had to close, and Dean Lane station, together with all the others on the line, closed on Saturday 3 October 2009. A number of special services, including steam-hauled trains, ran on the last day to celebrate the line and its history, and many local people turned out to watch the last trains run. The last service to depart from Dean Lane was the 23.25 Manchester Victoria to Rochdale train. Demolition of the station began almost immediately, and by the end of May 2010 there was almost nothing left.

The railway through Dean Lane remains open as a single-track branch serving the Dean Lane household waste facility. The Metrolink tram route to Rochdale runs parallel with it at Dean Lane, also as a single-track line.

SPELLOW (1882)

Date opened	September 1882
Location	East side of County Road
Company on opening	London & North Western Railway
Date closed to passengers	31 May 1948
Date closed completely	31 May 1948
Company on closing	British Railways (London Midland Region)
Present state	Station building survives in use as a bookmakers
County	Lancashire
OS Grid Ref	SJ356945

Spellow station was situated on the Bootle branch of the London & North Western Railway (LNWR), which ran from Edge Hill via the northern suburbs of Liverpool to the docks. The line was primarily intended to cater for goods traffic, and opened from Edge Hill to Stanley on 1 June 1866 and through to Canada Dock on 15 October 1866. Initially passenger services only ran as far as Tue Brook, south of Spellow, but in 1870 the LNWR extended the service through to Canada Dock. On 5 September 1881 a further branch was opened from the Bootle branch, just east of Canada Dock station, to Alexander Dock, which also carried passenger services.

At Walton, north of Liverpool, the Bootle branch passed under County Road, the main

Spellow, 1947

Liverpool to Preston road, in a deep cutting. By the 1880s Walton had developed from a small village into a residential suburb of Liverpool, and to serve the rapidly expanding area the LNWR opened Spellow station on County Road in September 1882.

The station had a street-level building that straddled the line on the east side of County Road. It was single-storey with a pitched roof, and the main entrance door in the centre led into the booking hall. At the rear of the building a set of covered

Spellow. *Stations UK*

Spellow: The station booking office was at street level on the east side of County Road, and in this view from July 1969 it was in use as a furniture store. The roof sign actually dated back to LNWR days, and underneath 'Kelly's Furnishers' was the original station nameboard; it survived until the early 1980s. *Nick Catford*

steps led down to a covered footbridge, which in turn gave access to the platforms. The line was double track so the station was provided with two platforms. The cutting through which the line ran at Spellow was carved out of sandstone rock, and both platforms were provided with canopies attached to the rock faces.

From its opening Spellow station was served by eastbound trains to Liverpool Lime Street and westbound services to both Canada and Alexandra docks. Services were

well used by dock workers as the line provided a direct link from the Walton area to the docks. However, the route to Liverpool Lime Street from Spellow was anything but direct. Trains travelled east, then turned south before finally heading west into the centre of Liverpool; the journey was nearly 6 miles, while by road it was only 2 miles. Horse-drawn trams were introduced to Walton in the late 1860s, and by 1902 the tramway had been electrified, providing a much better service to Liverpool than the LNWR could offer. However, the passenger services from Spellow continued to offer a good service to the outer suburbs and to the docks, although they were vastly outnumbered by a steady stream of goods trains.

On 1 January 1923 the Bootle branch became part of the London Midland & Scottish Railway (LMS). In the summer of 1932 there were five trains from Spellow to Canada Dock, 12 to Alexandra Dock and 17 to Liverpool Lime Street on weekdays. The first departure from Spellow was for Alexandra Dock at 6.49am, and the last was also for Alexandra Dock, at 10.39pm.

On 28 August 1940 Liverpool suffered its first bombing raid of the Second World War and in the following months the city suffered greatly. The Canada Dock branch was of national strategic importance, so was targeted by the Luftwaffe, but many of the bombs that were aimed at the line fell on the residential area around Spellow station. In very heavy raids on 4 May 1941 the Leeds & Liverpool Canal was hit at Canada Dock station; it flooded the station and passenger services were

Spellow: By February 2005 the booking office had found a use as a betting office. *Paul Wright*

Spellow: In this view of the westbound platform at Spellow in July 1969 the deep cutting in which the station stood is clearly illustrated. *Nick Catford*

withdrawn. Although the station was brought back into use for goods, it did not reopen for passenger services, leaving Spellow station with a service between Alexandra Dock and Liverpool Lime Street.

Upon nationalisation on 1 January 1948 Spellow station became part of the London Midland Region of British Railways, which withdrew the Alexandra Dock to Liverpool Lime Street service on 31 May of that year, and all the passenger stations on the route, including Spellow, were closed; Spellow had never had goods facilities, so closed completely.

Following closure the street-level station building was used as various retail outlets, including a furniture store and, in more recent

Spellow: Looking west in March 2008, the rear of the street-level booking office on County Road can be seen. The picture was taken from an elevated position made possible by scaffolding that had been erected as part of the Arnott Street School refurbishment works. *Paul Wright*

years, a bookmakers. The station infrastructure at track level fell into a state of disrepair and the footbridge and station canopies had been removed by the early 1960s. The platforms remained extant.

Meanwhile the line remained busy with goods services, and a passenger service that consisted of through coaches from Southport to London Euston that were joined to, or taken off, Liverpool and London services at Edge Hill. The through coaches were replaced by a DMU service in the mid-1960s, and this continued to operate until 9 October 1977. Freight traffic passing through Spellow station declined to its lowest in the late 1970s. In 1982 Canada Dock closed to goods services, but this was compensated for by the fact that from 1980 container services began to operate to the north docks. In the second half of the 1980s trainloads of imported coal started to use the line, followed

Spellow: Looking east from the westbound platform in March 2008, the remains of both platforms can be clearly seen. *Paul Wright*

in the 1990s by scrap metal. In 2011 the line through Spellow station was once again a busy freight route to the north Liverpool docks.

ALTCAR & HILLHOUSE (1884)

Date opened	1 September 1884
Location	South side of B5195 near present sewage works
Company on opening	Southport & Cheshire Lines Extension Railway
Date closed to passengers	7 January 1952
Date closed completely	7 July 1952, except for private siding until May 1960
Company on closing	British Railways (London Midland Region)
Present state	Demolished
County	Lancashire
OS Grid Ref	SD349061

Altcar & Hillhouse station was located on the Southport & Cheshire Lines Extension Railway (S&CLER), which ran from the north end of the North Liverpool Extension Line of the Cheshire Lines Committee (CLC) at Aintree to Southport Lord Street. It was promoted by local entrepreneurs who had initially tried to persuade CLC to build it. The CLC, which was a joint company made up of the Great Northern Railway (GNR), the Manchester, Sheffield & Lincolnshire Railway (MSLR) and the Midland Railway (MR), did not want to commit to such a scheme, but it did agree to work the line should it be built. It was intended that the line would tap into the lucrative holiday market for Southport as an alternative to the Lancashire & Yorkshire Railway (LYR) route to the town.

Altcar & Hillhouse station opened with the line on 1 September 1884, and was located about a mile west of Downholland on the south side of a road overbridge that carried what became the B5195 road over the line. The line was double track from the start so the station was provided with two platforms. The main station building, a brick-built structure that contained single-storey passenger facilities and a two-storey station master's house, was located on the northbound platform, and a small wooden shelter-type waiting room was provided on the southbound one. The station was also provided with goods facilities, which included sidings south of the station on the west side of the line.

At the time of opening Altcar & Hillhouse station was served by passenger trains operated by the CLC. The CLC had coaches of its own but had no locomotives, agreement having been reached among the partners that the MSLR would provide the motive

Altcar & Hillhouse, 1947

Altcar & Hillhouse: This view is looking south from the Wood Lane overbridge in 1949 and shows the passenger station and the goods yard that lay to its south. *John Mann collection*

power. Services operated to Southport Lord Street, Liverpool Central and Manchester Central, and excursions also passed through the station.

On 2 September 1887 the Liverpool, Southport & Preston Junction Railway (LSPJR) began operating a service from Southport Central to Altcar & Hillhouse, using a line that connected with the S&CLER just north of the station at what became Hillhouse Junction. The new service consisted of six trains per day, but it ran through very sparsely populated areas and by 1897 was down to four trains per day. In that year the Lancashire & Yorkshire Railway

(LYR) took over this route, and by 1901 it had diverted the service to run into Southport Chapel Street. In 1906 the LYR introduced a railmotor service on this route, which became known as the 'Altcar Bob' and did succeed in securing extra business.

On 1 January 1917 Altcar & Hillhouse station, together with all the stations on the line north of Aintree, closed to passengers as a wartime economy measure, not reopening until 1 April 1919.

At the time of the Grouping in 1923 the S&CLER remained independent, as from the beginning it had always really just an

Altcar & Hillhouse: On 6 June 1959 a rail tour was the very last passenger service to use the station. In this view looking south the station still had its main building on the northbound platform and the wooden waiting shelter on the southbound, although very overgrown, having closed in January 1952. *Bevan Price*

extension of the CLC. The CLC also remained independent, but its joint owners became the London & North Eastern Railway (LNER), which held two-thirds of the shares, and the London Midland & Scottish Railway (LMS), which held one-third. The LNER provided the motive power.

In 1926 the LMS, which had taken over the LYR, cut back the 'Altcar Bob' service to Downholland, more than a mile north of Altcar & Hillhouse. This left only the services to Manchester and Liverpool and ended the station's status as an interchange point.

In the summer of 1932 Altcar & Hillhouse had ten weekday trains to Southport Lord Street and 12 in the southbound direction, mostly to Manchester Central with a couple going to Liverpool Central. The route from Liverpool Central to Southport Lord Street was long and circuitous at more than 31 miles, while the LYR route from Liverpool Exchange to Southport Chapel Street was only 18½ miles, and had been electrified since 1904. The CLC was therefore in no position to compete for central Liverpool to Southport business.

For a period in late 1940 and the

early part of 1941 the line through Altcar & Hillhouse saw a much enhanced passenger train service. The reason was that the Liverpool end of the former LYR route between Liverpool Exchange and Southport Chapel Street had suffered major bomb damage, rendering it unusable for months. As a result extra services were laid on between Liverpool Central and Southport Lord Street.

On 1 January 1948 Altcar & Hillhouse became part of the nationalised British Railways (London Midland Region), which considered the line to be a financial liability and withdrew passenger services between Aintree and Southport Lord Street on 7 January 1952. Altcar & Hillhouse station remained open for public goods services until 7 July, after which they were withdrawn and the line north of the station was lifted. Train services continued to run to Altcar to serve private sidings south of

Right: **Altcar & Hillhouse:** This was the scene looking south in 1967. The last goods services had run in 1960 and the line was lifted shortly afterwards. *Tony Graham*

Below: **Altcar & Hillhouse:** Looking north in December 2005 nothing remained of the station. *Paul Wright*

the station, on what was now effectively a branch from Aintree to Altcar & Hillhouse. On 6 June 1959 an enthusiasts' special visited Altcar & Hillhouse station, the last time that passengers would ever use it. The private sidings closed in May 1960 and the line was lifted shortly afterwards. The station survived until the late 1960s, after which it was demolished.

In the 1990s the route of the line through the station site was developed as the Trans Pennine Trail cycleway and footpath.

LOWTON ST MARY'S (1884)

Date opened	1 April 1884
Location	South side of Newton Road
Company on opening	Manchester, Sheffield & Lincolnshire Railway
Date closed to passengers	2 November 1964
Date closed completely	22 April 1968
Company on closing	British Railways (London Midland Region)
Present state	Demolished
County	Lancashire
OS Grid Ref	SJ633976

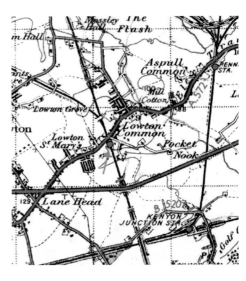

Lowton St Mary's, 1947

In 1874 the Cheshire Lines Committee (CLC) promoted the idea of a Wigan Junction Railway that would run from its main Liverpool to Manchester line at Glazebrook to the lucrative Lancashire coalfields. The CLC was a joint company owned by the Great Northern Railway (GNR), the Manchester, Sheffield & Lincolnshire Railway (MSLR) and the Midland Railway (MR). During the mid-1870s the railway was expanding rapidly at great cost, and the GNR and MR lost interest in the Wigan Junction Railway idea. The MSLR, however,

pressed on alone and received authorisation to build the line, which opened from an east-facing junction at Glazebrook to Wigan for goods services on 16 October 1879.

Lowton St Mary's station opened as Lowton on 1 April 1884, when passenger services were introduced to the line. The line was double-

Lowton St Mary's: This busy scene was brought about by a visiting rail tour in September 1956. Looking south, the picture gives a clear view of the station and its timber-built facilities. *John Mann collection*

track and the station was provided with two platforms. Located on the south side of a road overbridge that carried the Newton Road across the line, the main access was via a sloping driveway that led down from the road on the east side of the railway. The station was described as having only basic wooden facilities.

At the time of opening Lowton station was served by trains that ran between Manchester Central and a temporary station at Wigan. This was eventually replaced on 3 October 1892 by a new facility that was named Wigan Central.

On 1 July 1895 a line opened from a new junction just north of Lowton station to St Helens. It was built by the Liverpool, St Helens & South Lancashire Railway (LSH&SLR), and at the time of opening was only used by goods services. On 1 August 1897 the MSLR renamed itself as the Great Central Railway (GCR). The London & North Western Railway (LNWR) also had a station called Lowton, so to distinguish between the two the GCR station was often unofficially called Lowton Great Central.

The LSH&SLR had from the beginning wanted to operate passenger services and commenced a programme to upgrade the line. In anticipation of the new service, which would make Lowton a junction station, it was rebuilt. A single-storey timber building on the southbound platform contained the booking office and the usual passenger facilities, and a footbridge at the north end of the station provided access to the northbound platform, which was also provided with a single-storey

timber building.

Train services began running between Manchester Central and St Helens Central on 3 January 1900. Lowton had four trains to Manchester and five to St Helens, the services being operated by the GCR. In July 1900 a new north-to-west curve was put in at Glazebrook, which allowed trains to travel to and from the Liverpool direction on the CLC main line. On 1 January 1906 the GCR took over the LSH&SLR.

On 1 January 1923 Lowton became part of the London & North Eastern Railway (LNER), which changed the pattern of passenger services so that most northbound trains went to St Helens Central, and passengers for Wigan Central changed to a local service at Lowton.

On 1 January 1948 Britain's railways were nationalised and Lowton became part of British Railways (London Midland Region). BR renamed the station as Lowton St Mary's in order to avoid confusion between it and the former LNWR Lowton station. The St Helens service had been loss-making for years so BR withdrew it on 3 March 1952 and Lowton St Mary's lost its status as a junction station. In the BR era services ran from Lowton St Mary's to Wigan Central, to Manchester Central and to Irlam, where connections could be made for Manchester Central.

In the early 1960s diesel multiple units (DMUs) were introduced onto the line, but in the *Reshaping of Britain's Railways* report of 1963, the 'Beeching Report', passenger services on the Wigan Junction line were recommended for withdrawal. This subsequently took place with effect from 1 November 1964 and Lowton St Mary's station was closed. Goods services continued to run through to the St Helens line, but only as far as Haydock. On 22 April 1968 the line through Lowton St Mary's closed completely and was lifted shortly afterwards. The station's platforms remained extant into the 1970s, but eventually the site was developed as an industrial estate and all traces of it were swept away.

Lowton St Mary's: This early 1960s view is looking towards the east as a Wigan Central service pulls into the station. *John Mann collection*

Lowton St Mary's: Looking north in 1962, a goods train passes through the station. At the end of the northbound platform can be seen junction signals; the left-hand arm refers to the St Helens Central branch, while the right-hand arm is for the line to Wigan Central. *Bevan Price*

Lowton St Mary's: A rail tour visits in September 1963. *Bevan Price*

Lowton St Mary's: The derelict and overgrown station is seen looking north on 28 August 1976. The bridge that carried Newton Lane over the line had been strengthened by this time but would eventually be demolished. *John Mann collection*

Lowton St Mary's: The site of the station is seen in December 2005 looking south from the site of Newton Lane overbridge. *Paul Wright*

BLACON (1890)

Date opened	31 March 1890
Location	East side of Saughall Road
Company on opening	Manchester, Sheffield & Lincolnshire Railway
Date closed to passengers	9 September 1968
Date closed completely	9 September 1968
Company on closing	British Railways (London Midland Region)
Present state	Demolished; small section of platform ramp extant
County	Cheshire
OS Grid Ref	SJ384682

Blacon, 1947

Blacon station was situated on the Chester Northgate to Hawarden Bridge line of the Manchester, Sheffield & Lincolnshire Railway (MSLR), which opened on 31 March 1890 and provided a connection to the Wrexham, Mold & Connah's Quay Railway (WMCQR), which ran from Wrexham to Shotton. The MSLR had to bridge the River Dee at what became Hawarden Bridge to make a connection with the WMCQR line. With the opening of the MSLR line a route between Chester and Wrexham had been created that could compete with the 1846 Great Western Railway (GWR) route between the two towns.

A Chester avoiding line was built to the east of Blacon so that trains could travel through the city and onto the Cheshire Lines Committee (CLC) Chester-Manchester line without having to reverse at Chester Northgate. However, the avoiding line was mostly used by goods and

Blacon: In October 1950 station staff are applying a fresh coat of white paint to the edge of the westbound platform. Neither is wearing any form of high visibility clothing, which did not become common until the 1970s. *John Mann collection*

Blacon: The mock-Tudor station building stood on the westbound platform and was still present when this picture was taken on 3 April 1977. *Alan Young*

excursion services.

Blacon station opened at the same time as the line. The line was double-track and the station, which was on the east side of an overbridge that carried Saughall Road across the line, was provided with two platforms. Access was via a driveway that led to a two-storey brick and half-timbered station building designed in the Tudor style, which was located on the westbound platform on the south side of the line. The eastbound platform was provided with a simple waiting shelter. At the time of opening Blacon was served by four trains in each direction between Chester Northgate Station and Wrexham Central.

On 16 March 1896 the MSLR and WMCQR opened a line from Hawarden Bridge to a junction with the Wirral Railway (WR) at Bidston, and agreement was reached with the WR that MSLR/WMCQR trains could operate onto its system. On 18 May 1896 a passenger service was introduced between Chester Northgate and Bidston, and on 1 May 1898 it was extended to Seacombe & Egremont on the banks of the River Mersey, where a ferry terminal offered a service to Liverpool. The new service therefore provided Blacon passengers with a link to Liverpool.

On 1 August 1897 the MSLR changed its name to the Great Central Railway (GCR). On 1 January 1905 the GCR absorbed the WMCQR, giving it complete control of the entire route to Wrexham and to Birkenhead. On weekdays in 1906 five trains per day ran to Seacombe & Egremont, and more services ran to Wrexham Central; in the eastbound direction all trains went to Chester Northgate.

On 1 January 1923 Blacon station became part of the London & North Eastern Railway (LNER), but the service patterns remained the same. On 1 January 1948 the railways were nationalised, and Blacon became part of the London Midland Region of British Railways. It continued to be served by trains to Seacombe & Egremont, to Wrexham Central and to Chester Northgate. On 4 January 1960 the Seacombe service was diverted to run to and from New Brighton.

Because of the development of housing estates at Blacon the station remained busy during the 1960s and trains still ran to Chester, Wrexham and New Brighton. Diesel multiple units (DMUs) were introduced in the early 1960s but there were still occasional steam workings right up until 1966.

The *Reshaping of Britain's Railways* report of 1963, the so-called 'Beeching Report', recommended the withdrawal of all services from Blacon. However, a year later the station still had 14 weekday services to Wrexham Central, 12 to Shotton High Level, six to New Brighton and 32 to Chester Northgate. The first weekday service from Blacon in the summer of 1964 was the 5.28am to Wrexham Central, and the last weekday service was the 11.25pm to Chester Northgate.

Despite local protest services from Chester Northgate to New Brighton and to Wrexham were withdrawn on 9 September 1968 and Blacon station closed completely. The line continued in use as a goods line between Hawarden Bridge Junction and Mickle Trafford until 20 April 1984. The station survived until this time, although the main building was demolished some time before 1986. On 31 August 1986 the line reopened, again only for goods services; it was now a single track, and at Blacon only the former eastbound line was

Right: **Blacon:** Looking east in July 1980, the station had been closed for more than a decade but both of its platforms and the station building could still be seen. The line was still used for freight services, many of which served the Shotton steelworks. *John Mann collection*

Below: **Blacon:** Looking east 25 years later in April 2005, platform edge paving from the westbound platform's east-end ramp can be seen to the right of centre. By this date the route of the line through Blacon had been converted into a footpath and cycleway. *Paul Wright*

retained. The reopening was short-lived and the line was closed again in June 1992. It was 'mothballed' for a while, but was lifted before the end of the century. In 2000 a footpath and cycleway was opened along the course of the line, which at Blacon runs along the site of the former Chester-bound platform.

ASHTON-IN-MAKERFIELD (1900)

Date opened	3 February 1900
Location	West side of Lodge Lane (A49)
Company on opening	Liverpool, St Helens & South Lancashire Railway
Date closed to passengers	1 March 1952.
Date closed completely	4 January 1965
Company on closing	British Railways (London Midland Region)
Present state	Demolished
County	Lancashire
OS Grid Ref	SJ577983

Ashton-in-Makerfield station was situated on the St Helens Central branch, which left the Glazebrook to Wigan Central line at Lowton St Mary's. This line had been sanctioned as early as July 1885 and the original intention was to create a line that would link Wigan with Southport by creating a route from Lowton St Mary's to Fazakerley Junction on the North Liverpool Extension Line of the Cheshire Lines Committee (CLC). The company formed to build the line was the St Helens & Wigan Junction Railway (SH&WJR), which became the Liverpool, St Helens & South Lancashire Railway (LSH&SLR) on 26 July 1889, but it was in constant financial difficulty and, despite the first sod being cut on 28 January 1888,

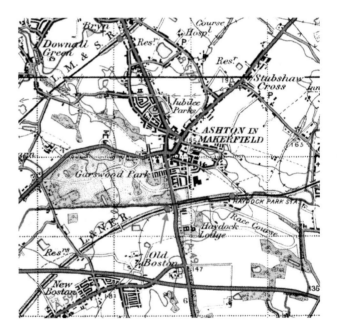

Ashton-in-Makerfield, 1947

Ashton-in-Makerfield: In the late 1940s it looks every inch the typical wayside station, and in this view looking west it appears to be very well cared for. At this time the staff would have had very little to do other than keep the station tidy and tend to the gardens as there were only a handful of passenger services. *John Mann collection*

Right: **Ashton-in-Makerfield:** In 1961 a train heads west through the station. Although passenger services between Lowton St Mary's and St Helens Central had been withdrawn in 1952, goods services continued to operate until the line between Ashton-in-Makerfield and St Helens Central closed in 1964 from a point a short distance to the west of the station. *Bevan Price*

the line did not open to goods traffic until 1 July 1895, and even then only from Lowton to St Helens. It would take another five years for the line to be brought up to passenger standards, by which time any hope of continuing westwards had been abandoned.

Ashton-in-Makerfield station opened on 3 February 1900; it was built to serve the township of that name, which lay to the north, but it was actually within the boundary of Haydock. It was situated on the west side of Lodge Lane, later the A49, which passed over the line on a bridge. A single-storey brick building on the south side of the line provided the main entrance and booking office, and because the line through the station was double-track it was provided with two platforms, both of which had brick-built waiting facilities. The station was also provided with a goods yard behind the westbound platform, which ran up to the rear of the main station building. The yard had a goods shed and three sidings; unusually the sidings were at a higher elevation than the passenger platforms.

Above: **Ashton-in-Makerfield:** By the date of this view, looking west on 28 August 1976, the station had been closed for more than 10 years, but it was still clearly recognisable as a former passenger station. During the 1970s and through to the late 1980s freight services to a scrap yard and an oil terminal continued to pass through. *John Mann collection*

Passenger services were provided by the Great Central Railway (GCR), which had invested money in the line. There were six trains in each direction. In the westbound direction all trains went to St Helens Central. Five of the eastbound services ran through

to Manchester Central and one terminated at Lowton St Mary's. Ashton-in-Makerfield station was situated close to the Haydock Park racecourse and from the start it handled race-day excursions even though a station was opened to the east inside the grounds of the course.

On 1 January 1906 Ashton-in-Makerfield

Right: **Ashton-in-Makerfield:** Looking west in December 2005, the station site had been developed as a business park. *Paul Wright*

Below: **Ashton-in-Makerfield:** Another view, looking east in January 2011. *Paul Wright*

station became part of the GCR when the LSH&SLR was absorbed by that company. At the Grouping of 1923 the line became part of the London & North Eastern Railway (LNER), which began to run additional services between Manchester Central and St Helens Central.

On 1 January 1948 the railways were nationalised and Ashton-in-Makerfield station became part of the London Midland Region of British Railways. Although the line had proved to be remunerative in terms of goods, passing through an area of numerous collieries, it never lived up to expectations with regards to passenger services. As a result BR withdrew

the passenger service from the line on 1 March 1952 and Ashton-in-Makerfield station was closed to passenger traffic, although it continued to handle race-day excursions throughout the 1950s.

On 4 January 1965 the line from St Helens Central to Ashton-in-Makerfield closed completely and was lifted to a point several hundred metres west of the latter station. In August 1968 a diesel multiple unit brought passengers to Ashton-in-Makerfield on a rail tour called the 'Makerfield Miner'. During the same year a connection was made with the West Coast Main Line, over which the St Helens and Lowton line passed; this allowed closure of the route through Lowton St Mary's to Glazebrook.

In 1975 the last racecourse excursions visited Ashton-in-Makerfield, but an oil terminal and a scrap metal company remained rail-served until the late 1980s. The remaining section of the former St Helens and Lowton St Mary's branch closed in 1991 and was lifted shortly thereafter. The station platforms remained extant until the whole site was redeveloped as office accommodation in the early part of the present century.

FORD (1906)

Date opened	1 June 1906
Location	East side of Netherton Way
Company on opening	Lancashire & Yorkshire Railway
Date closed to passengers	2 April 1951
Date closed completely	2 April 1951
Company on closing	British Railways (London Midland Region)
Present state	Demolished
County	Lancashire
OS Grid Ref	SJ354975

Ford station was located on the North Mersey branch of the Lancashire & Yorkshire Railway (LYR), which ran from Fazakerley Junction, on the Liverpool Exchange to Wigan Line, to Gladstone Dock. The line was opened in August 1867 as an important goods line linking the north Liverpool docks with the LYR route to the east. Connections from the North Mersey branch to the LYR Liverpool-Ormskirk line were provided at Sefton Junction (Aintree), travelling from west to north, and to the LYR Liverpool-Southport line at North Mersey Branch Junction (Litherland), travelling east to south.

In 1906 the LYR electrified the North Mersey branch from North Mersey Branch Junction to Aintree Sefton Arms and opened two stations at Linacre Road and Ford. Ford station opened on 1 June 1906 and was located on the east side of what became Netherton Way, which passed over the line on a bridge. The main line was double-track but there were also numerous sidings at Ford, forming part of the huge Aintree sorting sidings complex. The station was provided with two timber-built platforms; the eastbound platform had a simple timber waiting shelter, and a footbridge provided a link to the westbound platform, which was sandwiched between the main line and the area of sidings and which also had a simple wooden waiting shelter.

At the time of opening Ford station was served by an electric commuter service that ran between Aintree Sefton Arms and Liverpool

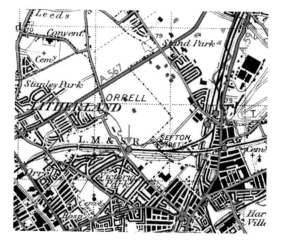

Ford, 1947

Exchange, calling at all stations en route. On 7 September 1914 the LYR extended the electrification from North Mersey Branch Junction to Gladstone Dock, where a new station was opened. From that date Ford station was therefore also served by trains running between Aintree Sefton Arms and Gladstone Dock.

At the west end of the North Mersey branch a connection had been made with the Liverpool Overhead Railway (LOR) in May 1905, and the LOR started to operate a service to Aintree Sefton Arms in 1906, calling at Ford. This provided passengers with a route that served all of the Liverpool docks and through to Dingle in the south of the city. The service

Ford: The only known view of the station was taken by the General Manager of the Liverpool Overhead Railway, W. L. Box, on Grand National day in 1930. This view looking east shows an LOR train passing through Ford on its way from Aintree Sefton Arms to Dingle. As can be seen, the station was constructed from timber and had only basic facilities. *Stations UK*

Ford: This is the view looking east from the end of the station in 1964. The station had been demolished five years earlier, but the large Aintree sorting sidings area was still in situ. In the distance to the left of the picture can be seen Sefton Junction signal box, which controlled the junction of the spur that ran between the North Mersey branch and Aintree Sefton Arms. The box closed on Sunday 13 April 1986 and was replaced by a ground frame. *J. R. Rimmer, Tony Graham collection*

was short-lived, however, ending in September 1908. However, on Grand National day every year LOR trains once again ran through Ford station as a special service was operated for race-goers.

On 1 January 1922 the LYR merged with the London & North Western Railway (LNWR), then a year later, on 1 January 1923, that company was in turn merged into the London, Midland & Scottish Railway (LMS). The LMS withdrew the Gladstone Dock service on 7 July 1924, leaving Ford with only the services to Liverpool Exchange and Aintree Sefton

Arms. In the summer of 1932 the LMS provided Ford with 22 trains to Liverpool Exchange and 20 to Aintree Sefton Arms. The first train was for Liverpool Exchange and departed from Ford at 6.17am; the last was also for Liverpool Exchange and departed at 10.21pm.

On 1 January 1948 Ford station became part of the nationalised British Railways (London Midland Region). BR discontinued the electric service through Ford on 2 April 1951 and the station closed completely. However, the line remained electrified for the movement of rolling stock and to allow the LOR Grand National services to run once a year. They ceased in 1956 when the LOR was closed in its entirety, but passenger services from beyond the Liverpool area still continued to pass through Ford on Grand National day.

The demolition of Ford station was completed on 1 May 1959, leaving no trace of it. The North Mersey branch had been built with the primary purpose of moving goods and it remained an important freight artery to and from the Liverpool docks until the mid-1960s, when the decline began. On 2 February 1971 the route of the line from North Mersey Branch Junction to the docks closed, then on 1 May 1977 the link with the Wigan line at Fazakerley Junction was also taken out. Only the section from North Mersey Branch Junction to Sefton Junction and to Fazakerley sidings, which was by then an engineer's depot, survived.

In the late 1960s a Freightliner depot known as the Aintree Container Base was built, the rail entrance to which was on

the site of Ford station's westbound platform. Since the 1960s the transport authorities in Merseyside had been developing plans to reopen the North Mersey branch, including Ford station, which was to be renamed as Giro, to passenger services. When the connection was laid into the depot space was left so that a station could be constructed. The connection to the depot opened on 13 July 1969, but it is believed that trains did not start running straight away. Goods trains serving the Metal Box factory at Aintree and engineer's trains to Fazakerley sidings also passed through the station site, and Grand National specials continued to pass until 1986.

On 19 February 1986 the Freightliner depot closed and on the 28th of that month the connection into the depot was taken out of use. With effect from 13 April the line through Ford station was singled. In 1987 the short spur to Fazakerley sidings was closed, and the Metal Box service had finished by 1991, leaving no regular goods services on the North Mersey branch.

The line through Ford still survived in 2011 as a route by which engineer's trains could access the Merseyrail Ormskirk line. The plan to reopen the line to passenger services was still an aspiration of Merseytravel in 2011.

Ford: The area seen here looking east in July 2005 had once been a mass of railway lines and sidings. The wooden station had been located in the foreground, and to the right of the line and stretching well into the distance is where the Aintree sorting sidings had once been. They had been taken out of use by 1969 and were replaced by a container depot, which in turn closed in 1986. The main line was also singled in that year. *Paul Wright*

Ford: This is the site of Ford station looking west in January 2011. By this date the line had no regular traffic, being used only by engineer's trains as a means of accessing Merseyrail's Liverpool-Ormskirk line. *Paul Wright*